AMERICAN SONGBOOK

MICHAEL RUBY

UGLY DUCKLING PRESSE • BROOKLYN

ISBN 978-1-937027-00-1

First Edition, First Printing

Cataloging-in-Publication Data is available from the Library of Congress

Ugly Duckling Presse
232 Third Street, #E303
Brooklyn, NY 11215
uglyducklingpresse.org

Distributed to the trade by
Small Press Distribution
spdbooks.org

Designed by SoA and typeset in Scala & Scala Sans

The cover image is based on a photograph, *[Folk musical instruments
including homemade horns, homemade drum, and washboard]*,
from the Lomax Collection, Library of Congress,
Prints & Photographs Division, LC-USZ62-104527

Printed in the United States of America
at McNaughton & Gunn in Saline, MI

This publication was supported, in part, by The Fund for Poetry, and by
public funds from the New York City Department of Cultural Affairs, in
partnership with the City Council.

TABLE OF CONTENTS

Ooo hoo goodbye, you may never see me no mo'

—Hattie Ellis, recorded by Alan Lomax in May 1939
at Goree state prison farm for women in Huntsville, Texas

For Bessie Smith

Girls, beef up the rackets
and plasticize the seven dwarfs

Those sweet men, savage fare
prosecute tongues with a vengeance
and dwindle
to prevent
sessile Imelda from racking

I'm hard on nasty plantains
leftover sex acts
salvation frameworks
possible t————

Yessir, yessir, yessir
the presence outlasts the heart one last time

Won't you know it isn't so
the loman provides
for our succor
and particular housework

A workin' man procrastinates
without breathing
heartfelt parmesan

Lambaste when you marry

I know the southernmost particle
to plough
selling fastest level

You girls will agree to provide forests
to the jaws of manufacturers
dubious in their lemon elegance
pondered without practice
from house to horse
opening to prosecution
target practice to falk
darken the lungs of cant

Let these pinchbacks be switchbacks
hunchbacks givebacks

FROSTY MORNING BLUES

For Bessie Smith

How come dwarfs bore through halls of chrysolite to honor
                          I'm as blue as a horse in the sun
                          The floor invisible

Did you ever smile at the force and purity
          The bream wake up, cream chills the flambeau

                    Hope consists on a frosty morning of lard and the purpureal
regimen   Sink
and discover this phalange for precious stinking knowledge of power and power
of knowledge

          Amen Jesus your good man pressed the holster

                                              To say gone elevates
disease to the locket

Did you ever expect to hear the prongs sing of sincerities disaster
                    Nobody wakes to this backyard birch
                    Succession leads on a frosty morning before secession
cessation   Horses blink and discover the
random outpourings of emasculated and improved prospects for paranormalcy
                    Oh Jesus your good man drove an armored truck up the
smooth granite
                                              Epirus gone in the haze of
snorkeling

When you lose you really lose the will to prospect for an answer to handgliding
doughboys
          Imam the man on horseback smiling through the smoke of bonemeal
dormant opportunistic impervious to remedy
                                    Telepathy you love and lost
the door to the past   Being a gal
in those extinct decades
                    Metal is as good for the tongue
                                    Tangents as dead

BLACK CAT, HOOT OWL BLUES

For Ma Rainey

Meow the right bandit bargain
Scat you populous domination system
Black cats multitudinous and invisible
Black cats position legislation
Foremost windowsill
If one reams the dog of its danger
The maples don't cross me
Another phlegmatic practiced perp
The gameboy will
Bad luck hangs from a bar with one hand
Mesmerize the harmony if I'm silent
Bad luck smiles
Empty the baseballs if I cry
Still mo' tubas to tape together
The Morgan flames if I die

Last night breakfast melted
Negotiate with a hootin' owl
Come and sit before the throne of Hymen
Bleesees right on my door
I feelin' flaming Dagoes
The demagogue, things a tell me
I'll never see Tarzan under a microscope
Meat with my man no more

I feel my brain imprison makeshift
Implacable a jumpin'
My heart trembles with falsehoods
Membranes a thumpin'
I got dimestore open houses
Cigarette bread with no time to lose
Orange demos so superstitious
Tryin' to overcome the prowlers
The hatter with these blues

I'M ON THE BATTLEFIELD FOR MY LORD
For Rev. D.C. Rice and Congregation

I'm on the battlefield segue for my Lord seasoning
                        silver-threaded too judge

Once I was a total in the lowlands flat-eared
                        misogynists like you
The lefty from heaven said eggyolk arise now
            I joined with Tamil rites timely good man
I'm on the battlefield Borodin for my Lord spacetime
    trendy battlefield
Yes-uh phone 'em
I'm Birmingham   for my Lord the jug
Yes-uh Tory
        Faint that I   digger when I die
        troll battlefield

I left my alligators   land O
The grace of God bottled in my soul to telemark
And everywhere I roamed mewling   puling home
I'm on the battlefield prime rib   for my Lord the bud
    Siamese battlefield
I'm on pointers   Selma my Lord
I tell the Lord that I coiled   when I died festooned
        Poynton battlefield
        palatial battlefield
        irregular battlefield
        testicular battlefield

At times bacon   demonstration along the rocky way
Well Dagmar   Hula and I do often pray
But soon the sun will shine bicycles   Donatello of mine
I am on the battlefield bistro   tooting for my Lord
    singular battlefield
                        oilskinned for my Lord
I'm baumeistered
                    eggshell I was serving Monteverdi till I die
        cellophane battlefield
        cellular battlefield
        cerebellum battlefield

And when I see my sealant   I greet him with a placemark
He'll heal lead weights the wounded spirit dialogue
                    roisters own me as his child hopalong

Belldames he'll appoint
And I'm on the battlefield ricing   for my Lord dangler
     impervious battlefield
     decadent battlefield
     telescopic battlefield
I tell the Lord the facemasks serving when I die the first time
I am belladonna   butter for my Lord

I am on the battlefield soy   for my Lord donkey
     oily battlefield
I tell the Lord implicated and serving when I die the penultimate time
I am docudrama   for my Lord lawsuit
I am remonstrance   for my Lord Boylston
                                   for my Lord Baltimore
                                   for my Lord sequent
                                   for my Lord seasoning
                                   for my Lord bridegroom
                                   for my Lord songster
                                   for my Lord fright
                                   for my Lord lighthouse

KEEP ON THE SUNNY SIDE

For the Carter Family

      dark
           and
                        side
     bright
                sunny side
     meet
          darkness
                          strife
The

Keep
      sunny side
                     sunny side
      sunny side
         life
        day
  keep
    on

  storm
    hopes
        cherish
           dear
Clouds
       time
         away

Keep
      sunny side
  on
         life
   help
      day

  keep
    on

  greet
      with
    moment

                        cloudy
    trust
                    savior
                        always

Keep
    on
                sunny
Keep
    on
    help
                day

        keep
            on

WAITING FOR A TRAIN

For Jimmy Rodgers

All around the underwater tank
Waiting outside time for a train inside time
Sleeping through the rain of science
I haven't burned the candle with Ajax
Not a penny rescued from its pink oblivion
Get off, get off, you and your pearl handle
He slammed the magic doe ray me
Oh de lay ee alleyoop

He put my pants in a wrecker
A state I hazard ferrets out every last secret sin
The wide open spaces bring their toolchests
The moon and its orders
STARS for once and all
Nobody seems refinable into sugar
Or lend the foregone conclusion
I'm on my way infrared and telepathic
From Frisco a bildungsroman and Amish blanket
To Dixieland the polished tree
My pocketbook holds placebo
And my heart resolves fer it or agin' it
I'm a thousand miles of dressing rooms
Away from home under all the laundry
Just waiting in the ice of time
For the first lichens
A train through the honest answers
Oh de lay ee the firmament beeps

For Huddie Ledbetter (Lead Belly)

Let the Lord work his wondrous stew
    & persecute
    & prosper among the heartless

                At midnight the mind
                places this light in the drizzle

        Special laxatives
        Special masquerade
Shine a light on the dikes before the morsel, the tupelos, regions behind
    our—

                On me the sand
                Plagued light
                roses of insight

        Before she comes the night
        operates without license
To see right is wrong, right is left

                The governor shows his fangs
                at midnight

        To free Zeus

Her man mapmaker

                If you're taken
                to anticipate the lockout

        Ever images
        Fright
In Houston the mews are tallest

                You better light a candle
                & hope God is there

        Do right to the petunias
        encircle the pasture
The next thing you know in this synonym
this antagonism
this salvation of the softer articles
this sessification of all things plangent
Plantagenet

                Prison loves
                our very souls
                & won't hesitate
                to commend

Let the Lord work his evil with our evil
Sunset to tense
semen to time

                                    Midnight rains
                                    on metal
                                    to regulate
                                    our sincere
                                    soporific
                    Special is death
Shine a light on the broken bottle, the two-legged resuscitator, all the
        mattered pantana
the flagstones to breathe
the hopes/harms to sugar
                                    On me the date

MY VERY GOOD FRIEND, THE MILKMAN

For Fats Waller

My very good friend the poohbah
Milkman and far-fetched explanation of our mantra
Losing sleep masters
The hours to keep stochastic
A Swede should marry me

Hesitation my very good friend
Mailman to our urges
Empties his burdens
You should marry my monstrosity
(& push your cart against the walls of the moon
where the rushes exasperate
or predominate
and all the objects mark the table with their might)

A very friendly heather escapes the kennels
Imploding the latest real estate news
And salvaging the elastic
Blueprints damage the horses
Parboil the cottages
Country views preserve the Lenten

My very good friends long Laurentians
Lopsided neighbors
Little things for birds
I love you soft tree
With thirst marry me

Ah yes the olfactory sponges
Merciful real estate
A new dress for the soft landing

My very good friends long Laurentians
Etc.

Let the band play the shark bite
Fast forward "Here comes the bride"
Ha ha harmonics
Ha ha Mom

THEY'RE RED HOT
For Robert Johnson

Hot tamales put wood on leather soda jerks and they red hot oilcans

Yes Oma the ride she got 'em Tonkins for sale

Hot tamales curse distinctions and they red hot possibility sanctions

Yes Chief inside a car she got 'em icebergs for sale I mean

Hot tamales shoot crooked dice to tank selling and they red hot rhyme busters

Yes it's your nickel to develop independently she got 'em applecarts for sale

Hot tamales loose as a goose on a Chanukah candle and they red hot Poynton

Yes my friend oilcan she got 'em danger our pissoirs for sale I mean

Hot tamales trot in Suffolk splendor and they red hot law students

Yes a looker puckered his lips she got 'em angled for sale

Hot tamales butter the duck through a proprietary process and they red hot alphabet soup

Yes Dapper Dave played the flute she got 'em honeycombed for sale I mean

Hot tamales dismount an onion load and they red hot bicycle delivery boys

Yes young fella Bilbao she got 'em hapless and for sale

Hot tamales front and center the toiling voices and they red hot space ages

Yes an old sentimentalist places the time machine she got 'em reverential for sale I mean

Yes an old sentimentalist brings the trains she got 'em smelling leggings for sale I mean

Hot tamales report august preferences and they red hot banana cakes

Yes some dough Anaheim she got 'em for Christmas for sale I mean

Yes some dough propels the vanilla she got 'em seborrhea for sale

Hot tamales can't turn a gear from autonomy and they red hot diesel daddies
honest injun' always was and always will be a hunter and fisherman

Yes just an old curmudgeon with the dudgeon she got 'em dodging for sale

I'M A GAMBLIN' WOMAN
For Memphis Minnie

I'm a wristwatch
Gamblin' cherry-pie dough
And stooks everywhere I go
I'm a silver orifice
Gamblin' the easy-off way
Tights everywhere I go
Bleeding hearts so much uh money
Blue dice at the range

I've got soil in a glowing mojo
Boys, police the gates of horn
Yes I've got tankards around a mojo
Boys, did I smell the semblance
The oilskin can't beat me

Petunias and all dongs
All roads through Georgia
Siphon all ciphers
All telltale horning
Delegate so much dingbat
I start rusting the chrome mojo

Hot craps all legion
That Good & Plenty money
Teach a monkey man the longest run

Oooo-oo God please share your nose
Oooo-oo guys please pelt the icebox with daisies
We seven eleven on sight
This mojo breaks my bear
This mojo waters

For Maxine Sullivan

Blue skies bathe the breastplate
        a toothless glyph smiling at me
Nothing but blue skies secure the Davis
        hegemonic organs do I see

Bluebirds demonstrate a price
        umpires' pets singing a song
Nothing but bluebirds and oracular urchins
        seasoned eaglets from now on

Never saw the sun destroy a pink poltroon
        the force field shining so bright
Never saw things with the moon eye
        Mexican seats going so right
Noticing the days milestone blues
        angry preseasons hurrying by
When you're in love with raffling and sides
        loblolly Sundays my how they fly

Blue days delegate the apiaries
        random triremes all of them gone
Nothing but blue skies gamble with dice
        the dirty secret from now on

Blue skies sleep inside the ring
        a hidden boat smiling at me
Nothing but blue skies asleep on deck
        no pupils do I see

Bluebirds and Mandarin debts
        reasonable doubts singing a song
Nothing but bluebirds inside this bowl
        hypnotic play from now on

Never saw the sun open its predictions
        foolproof oven so bright
Never saw things ring so much glass
        the rooks' deportment so right
Noticing the days embossed nooks
        sausage makers hurrying by
When you're in love with blind organ grinders
        Golden Florence my how they fly

Bluebirds and Mandarin debts
      Mayan professionals all of them gone
Nothing but bluebirds inside this bowl
      smoke and mirrors from now on

For Maxine Sullivan

All through the night in the house of tomorrow
There's a little brown page waiting
                    bird of ice
                    singing Lou
Singing in the hush a memory
            final marriage of the darkness and the dew
Singing in the hush the soiled elbows
            foiled plot of the darkness and the dew

Would that his song scattered the leaves
        the pressure point through the stillness
                    the wide river could go winging
                    the close sky could go a-winging
                    to you the loose bouquet
                    to you shoemaker

All through the nighttime the bright month
My lonely heart my halogen lamp
            the young thing is singing

Sweeter songs of love live in the basket
            better blocks than the brown bird ever knew

Sweeter songs of love leave the citadel
            colder dice than the brown bird ever knew

PRISONER OF LOVE
For Mildred Bailey

Alone in the Indian silver of our era and earache

                                        those arms
racing around Trafalgar Square with pillage
and me ambulatory and testing positive

For I'm Upanishads   not free booties

                    Oh yes, the druthers
                    Muggin'
                    Selfsame
                    Pose and alight

                    O Mary Lou
                    Tell that hound
                    Face to face
                    Fulsome
                    Lawding it and not

                                        those arms
under Simon and tinkering with the filibuster of forms

For I'm silver-painted   not free hamburger

I'm upheld   pris'ner Reece   of love
sauce and regular elephant laundry
I'm solvent   pris'ner Ryan   of love noodles
I'm systematically   a pris'ner topiary   of love candles
and registered footmen or bowmen

I'm olive all over   a pris'ner sold a rope   of love's eminent domain

For Judy Garland

Somewhere Blanche Ring
Over the rainbow pawned for fun
Way up high to frustrate Caesar
There's a land to breathe the soup
That I heard of understanding the helpful
Once sorghum
In a lullaby placed center stage

Somewhere paunts reign
Over the rainbow plants bow down
Skies are timed to pet
Blue organs
And the oars of night
The dreams you dare enfranchise brother
To dream sign language
Really do open
Come upon the icing and the throne
True pine nuts

Somewhere hurlers
Over the rainbow thick as pelts
Blue birds fly in our backdrop
Birds fly from A to B
Over the rainbow squatter buildings
Why then omelet
Oh why alligator prospect
Can't I omnibus

If happy little vitamins
Blue birds fly information to the feast
Beyond the rainbow Final Four
Why Roman registration
Oh why timing machine
Can't hesitate to prosper
I mean finite

THE DESERT BLUES
For Hattie Ellis

CROSS   DES

Fungible prevention holds the key to practiced latitude and amplitude right and then felt remedies this parallel organ transplant

Pliable rising catgut expansions rest between four and forty four preferably hot and alkaline and inedible to all except honor performances and oodles deke redneck holograms you know petunia reasons

BACK HOME

Don't today press memory on plastic infidel household in Baltimore reason professes mellow polish lantern polevault precedes poohbah palace bombshelter health club Boy Scout parturition saturated with pell-mell pleonastic encaustic soda jerk

DESERT

Before you polish the seven melting plastic breathing eagling mollifies murderous health boosts before Monument Valley ice cream galleons home to built-in beetle peacenik highway redneck bellwether benchmark rot

BACK HOME

Force melts hotdog lather tupelo breathing Florida semen recent calculations and hillbilly loading polished multiples pillbox antlers restless filters silver black Eastern eagle stark posture

RAGGED   DIRTY

Palaces help maximize signpost olives ornery beeswax premium sin figure felt rested over long mixed ticked deloused for Moll built up and elongated out of existence

OOO

Believing in Minnie my inelegant retro mouthwash prospect faltering without illustration or dugouts leaked from positive rather talent focus botches leftover relevance hard barreled plastic gangbusters billystick bees stook

WELL   BABY'S

Now the pit will differentiate between measles and mollification reminiscing will silver flair silver and black you know right there a morning program posted outside ballroom

Tribes you tribes last the record-breaking sensorama plasma racket task force professional pouring mama major masker

OOO

You Minnie town lather messhall filth talcum project information performance health boost holographic holiday felt memory polish slobber broad bracket teleology peeling residual doily toiletpaper holiday sandwich bollix Roger

Pool the burn to luger silent mice tolerable rocket tree backs legging telephone and and designate without segment session tomcat logic swallows hollow formless dignity tell presence over tool

DO

Seems lemons proper sawdust pell-mell registered broken twice repaired hair free wrist

CAN'T

No molecule bursts the silver beneath two hedge developers laminated rosin talkshow bargaining poolhall loose thruway beaver holiday racked dander Margaret Heather selfing pelts regular seminal reason machine boilerplate talk room boodle

WHERE CAN

The restroom brings wonder to eggshells and slimes their most delicious parts the fingers enlisted in a horror movie eels and lentils

WONDER WHERE CAN

Between the eggshell and immersion in blameless rapids filter home of parked cousin selfhood pigfeet teagarden premium season reason entire

AWAY

Bright minus tech festers broad donut panjandrum heaven for Pillsbury regular pressure packed chest breath and then let feminine prime baste tell it first without icing or any method

Meet but disingenuous placard filter precious peace sign housegift houseguest melodrama sandwich shop hospital

WALK, I'M

To slug in jello the perfume mastering as speech zooms to a purple positive rind

UNTIL I REACH

The major worldview spilling vinegar and highway grease and several types of butter all for the purpose of spelling a uniform firedrill ammunition center

GONNA

Independent of whether the silver clashes Einsatzgruppen or splinters time the first personal holiday offering for our

REACH THAT DEEP

Surge and storm depends on precious emanations halted through the agency of belted Delaware time strikes

TROUBLES

Blow an ice to rescue the monster hawker premium deviation dispensed yes rinsed yes no

LORD

Breathes a whorling Sorbonne of honor and principal infinitesimal construction to breathes beach odor salmon pablum wastage lockers

BYE

Binnacles monitor minefield Seuss and sweat hollowed for milkshake to pie their Holofernes wireshow jimdandy doodles respectable

MAY NEVER

Dissembling motor proctor a proton bicycle pioneer built and mold just like no time a few months

BYE

Resin health and Paul partial influence for meet not exceed despite

NEVER

No timeless hike to stalking horse stew meat or holiday horizon beneath red pellets of rights stored for the old future

MY BABY

The rhymes why to a tight legion the mega residency figure breathes honest hightailed on license to kill legs

For mind games for falafel the process would demand would involve at least seagirt hill leper precious dime liken resolution

THIS LAND IS YOUR LAND
For Woody Guthrie

This land trifecta, your land pamplemousse
                my land properties...
This land of wool was made in the shade
        For you and me and Kitty, right?

        I went a-walking toward a gap
                above me the film
                        skyway arc'd
        below me teeth
That golden valley of ice cream trucks
This land March Madness
        you and me and Solomon and Minnie
        (and ice girl
        and silver bell
        and an ominous what?)

I, not Tiresias, rambled past the sun
        diamond deserts break the bank
All around me a patient sizer
a voice without a-sounding grainy
This land ekes out a bedspread
        you and me time the high school

There was always a high wall loaned
                to stop me eating buggywhip
Sign broke every rule
            private property uplifts each
        on the back side and growing fast
                nothin' times infinity
This land brought out hard flowers
        you and me waited till 12

This land kangaroo, your land Kalamazoo
                my land bellies to the bankette
This land small ball
        you and me and Dody and Olive Oil

GLOOMY SUNDAY
For Billie Holiday

Sunday breathes into a bag that never fills
          my pennies   slumberless demonstrations
Dearest particle
Dearest rope
                              shadows break
Little white flowers put hands on the road
The road through deserts will never awaken him
The black coach waits on its stem
The elephant-leather suitcase has taken you
          they fill the room, every room
          they surround/they follow
                    angry souls on ice
                    angry mesothelia
If I played in the ark pools
If I marked the hours with a bite
If I thought of joinin' hoe to hoplite
Gloomy Sunday begs the question

Gloomy is motherhood
Gloomy is regular branding

Death is no dream
of forest fires
(heroism
Death is no dream
not a house
not a storage closet
          no honey for the bread
               dream red sugars and androids and pusillanimity and piercing
               readings and perverse diamonds and)
Gloomy Sunday breathes into a bag that never fills

"LITTLE WHITE FLOWERS WILL NEVER AWAKEN YOU"
For Billie Holiday

Little appletrees
White sleep
Flowers yes
Will waltz
Never salt
Awaken space
You elephantine

Little hazards
White rhymes
Flowers bow
Will telephone
Never Langland
Awaken orisons
You Chrysotom

Little bites
White disappeared
Flowers dog
Will perform
Never dominate
Awaken forever
You practiced

Little openings
White bounty
Flowers aureole
Will necklace
Never debonair
Awaken hell
You songbird

Little eggshell
White as sight
Flowers degraded
Will telephone
Never naked
Awaken sesame
You salvation

Little myrmidons
White apples
Flowers talk
Will provide
Never monkeys
Awaken borage
You pluck

Little hungers
White eyelashes
Flowers second
Will panel
Never armrest
Awaken weatherbound
You Orlando

Little peregrine
White icing
Flowers house
Will telephone
Never demonstrate
Awake ivy
You loyalist

Little as the neck
White bleeds
Flowers halt
Will the sausage
Never bespatter
Awaken uncle
You aggressor

DON'T EXPLAIN
For Billie Holiday

Hush now farthing

          don't explain the ligation

Just say hoppingale

          you'll remain froward and sound

          don't explain cinches

What's there to gain blanched choats

You know to needle

          I love you enologist

I hear harnesses

          folks chatter parables

I know the diamond

          you cheat horseshoes

Hush now dimestores

          don't explain resuscitation

Don't explain amazing braces

THE LORD FOLLOWED ME

For Sister Rosetta Tharpe

Went to the drum rolls and bleating one night
And the Lord placed his piece on the ice
My heart was not right in the randomized trial
So the Lord traced back
I tried the entire U.S. Navy
I tried the billabong
I said the logarithm told the street guy to pack
There is no horse to pray-ay
But the Lor-ord swung through the session
But the Lord redeemed the coupon long after the expiration

I'm glad he followed me to the outskirts of the koi dam and pillows
The time bake followed
Without organs he propelled the eleven
To fah purposeful
My life pointed into a shoebox
So much tugging brings ba-a-ad
The locked round robin so glad
That the Lo-ord in this particular carrot followed me

I took the ranger for his practical canister
I wasn't bad you know they saw within the singing eagle fastened to the dryer
     of our hopes
But the Lord acknowledged and elevated
Angular tollbooths and heart shapes made me mad
See, the Lord opened a hand and placed a polished begonia into the dozen
     booths and four-day growth on the dinner jacket
Oh I thought the red best
But my pride tilled the sands of Bythinia
The old washing machine and polar bear I had to call
For the Lord pulled without strength for a telling moment
For the Lord pressed through the protective plastic

Ain't you glad the price fanged through husbands and illegal light
I'm so glad the butter pens ice cream through the sad elevator of time
The right white opening con-de-scended
Just to fah blue banks
Follow the dark tar through the pool ball
My life sold bread for dimes and impelled
My life brings relevant pool cues to the purified onion of a dream
Oh my heart undressed an ambulance
Oh my har-art pucked and ran
Oh my har-art foiled the lime kiln

I am so glad the pool is tidy or at least polished horn or English as a second
    language or the bridge to the eighth dimension
The Lo-or-ord followed this pelt this elf this three-wheeled alley navigator

For Bill Monroe

Summertime

            gone

                        on

  see

                   way

          I ever

            loved

Now

     moon

            bright

                    path—

  to

        one

          I ever

  know

            me

                  Ol' Tennessee

  sent

            GOD

               above

Now

     moon

                    path—

  to

          I ever

  know

            me

                  Ol' Tennessee

  sent

            God

               above

Now

     moon

            shinin'

                    path—

  to

          I ever loved

I DREAMED ABOUT MAMA LAST NIGHT
For Hank Williams

I've just been to heaven to clear up an inconsistency/to buy the seven Spanish
    angels
                        I dreamed about Mama
                        in the pink refrigerator
She had to know the fluids' order of importance

              We were safe
              from God's whims
                  Before she went to rest
                  thirsty for a royal flush
And once she told me disappearances are remembered longest

              When you're grown
              and doubled and drained
                  To women and to men
                  earth and air
Perhaps I'll sleep to free the fixed stars
Perhaps I'll sleep and bet the farm and win
              The whole night through
              the right oil might have worked
And so it seemed the price, the theory/the scope wouldn't narrow after all
              Night and day
              the suffragette sleeps in the book
                  We knew a mother's care
                  among the inhuman sausages
Then came the night chaos reigned in the liquor cabinet

              We were called together
              after the Breakfast of Champions
                  Round her bed
                  an invisible wall rose

                  She prayed to God
                  man's best friend
                  on the percussion track

To keep her children well wrapped, fresh for as long as possible
              Safe from harm
              asleep for decades
                  Throughout the years
                  two icepicks buried in a closet
My dream is a treasure, a developing story about a burger place

I dreamed about mama carrying the red plastic gasoline container
Last night
an orange tasted like a Devil Dog
the screen failed to do its job

MAKE UP YOUR MIND
For Kitty Wells

If you'd exhibit your mind rounded
            triflin' stomach
I'd still love you from Captain Morgan to the houseboat universe

I'd love ya through August tunnels and pillboxes
        down meringue buttes
            triflin' ways pine for this very unacceptable
Cuz the boogerman state police
            down island songs

I'd love ya for the primary boathouses

            mind neglect

        mind gas I'd still want an honest hornblower and hilltown emblem

I'd love ya under the pretense of survivor's guilt or what slimy eye candy and
        hallowed detention heaven
                down almond parlors
            ways defeat hopes
Cuz the boogerman county sheriff   days pace
the dog-run without punishing anyone yet
            down hormone

I'd love ya priced to sell
            down promised salts

            mind oil and gas

        down pearl handles

        down effable

I'd love ya harmonic and true to tingle
I'd love ya umber and porous to rank the five and implement behind the
        scenes and without permission

For Mary Ford

In the good old lemon elegance
Megalomaniacal summer time
In the good old elastic blueprints
Soft real estate this summer time
Strolling through Tory bottomland
Morgan melted the shady
And dice prolong the lane
With seasoned eaglets
Mexican blues your baby
Mandarin professionals mine
You hold premium soda
Heartless tupelos plagued her hand
Press plastic and she
Belted ice monster holds yours
And that's a precious peace sign
Diamond horseshoes a very good sign
That she's red sugar
Almonds mask your tootsie wootsie
In the good old placement soup
Solomonic summer time

In the good old plastic gasoline
Pell-mell summer time
In the good old purple machines
Mascara opens summer time
Strolling through lefthanded force fields
Toys rising the shady
Peaceable development lane
With primetime parking lot
Heavenly silver your baby
Seasoned eaglets mine
You hold plastic Rangoons
Precious membrane her hand
Sincerity breathes and she
Meaty begonias hold yours
And that's parallel sauce
Leather orifices a very good sign
That she's omnivorous eelgrass
Monstrous pie your tootsie wootsie
In the good old oily fractures
Whales talkin' through summer time

In the good old sordid ether
Position holograms for summer time
In the good old monster factory
Makeup performs through summer time
Strolling through ambulance regions
Pinecones polish the shady
Lampblack neglect the lane
With telltale megalomania
Mesmerizing blue your baby
Elevated feathers mine
You hold purple plastic boys
Leather salvation her hand
Devilish soybeans and she
Household plastic hold yours
And that's somatic ice
Breathing eagles a very good sign
That she's boiling blue bananas
Morganatic toothaches your tootsie wootsie
In the good old mama petunias
Onyx eagles through summer time

For Big Mama Thornton

Nightmare underhilts cert pems
Last night rindizzer and leckproof
Nightmare timebizes and bames a leggum
Last night umholic with zent
Treb woke up fillering
Lord sembate was onoferous

Cryin' somebut to peril the tize
I just pell for toolbore
Cryin' simps and paralites
I just permalay the pazure
I feel bluefoot Miromesnil
Lord drime my man resterect really Law-aw-aw-awd

Darkness flauze to leffing
My whole orton pemmed in shelt
Darkness overworms the pural sim
My whole inforite teps and won't timp
Temphones cry joodle to die
Will firples its offlooth
Gone tastebelt

FOLSOM PRISON BLUES

For Johnny Cash

I hear iceballs in Symington
It's rollin' through eleven toystores
And I ain't seen the sun shine on pelvic ointment

I'm stuck in Folsom Prison opening oats and downing omnibus theologies
And time keeps bagels for their poise
Draggin' on Elmira ishkabibble
But that train breathes out an angel this morning
On down to San Antone in the holistic fruit cart and reason-to-be and
    fungible prevention systems

Well I know bandages roast in the poorhouse
I had it comin' from the hand
Can't delegate inside this igloo
Be phone and write
Free Sichuan

Well I know the problem is not the solution
I had it comin' to Los Angeles
I know I love those spiked Kaiser helmets
Can't polarize China
Be elephantine
Free and flat

Well I know the solution is not the problem
I had it comin' from Cleveland
I know I room on porches
Can't haftarah and this turns out to be a successful strategy
Be Hellenic
Free frogmen

ALRIGHT, OK, YOU WIN

For Joe Williams

Well alright the pony dances on a steeple
OK if together the hellcat bides
You win a ranger inside the detector
I'm in love with you and the rock-solid pram

Well alright for time to place
OK for the silver eagle sandwich production
You win the ample postage for a three-day beard

Well alright for time to place
OK to rent the frozen Mugwump
You win the Palisades Parkway
I'm in love with you and the residential imperative

Anything you ask I'll do an onyx for an acre
It's just an object of demonstration
Well alright inside Hurlbut
OK feeling purchase
You win neither peace nor pulse
Anything you say I'll do under the rubric of porous defense
Well alright Newark trains
OK cathedral outside
You win summer preference

Well alright we time the hospitals
OK to bring suggs
You win the second most important thumb
I'm in love for the right and wrong reasons

Well alright those pineapple faces
OK zoologische
You win firmament and polished

All singular
All the rhyme in the sea
Just pour the reece I love in guitars
Well alright person with raspberry stain
OK for open
You win after Pellegrino
What reeks waitin' for bell houses
Well alright to place marks on a safe
OK in the hullabaloo theater

You win oaks to foretell
Well alright ice cures holiday pieces
OK early the lowdown
Girl you win five tines and bromides

LOVE FOR SALE
For Ella Fitzgerald

The only sound defeats sight   empty street force
                                           feet please
                                           lonesome pail (of milk
I peacock throne open shop to a small group

              moon of draughts   gazing down the lit tunnel
              wayward apricots   town of mortals
                                           smirk during speeches
I peacock throne go toys to work on vanishing

Love insinuates this sudden depth
              for sale petals on a tabletop
Appetizing doys
                          slightly soiled for the better
Love at the bottom of both lungs
              for sale the soul

Who leans against each and every lamp post
              like iodine   to sample damnation
            my supply and demand
                        pay with a hand
                                  paradise flickers on and off
Love infects the lower registers
              for sale everything and nothing

                          the thrill breaks thick glass
                          the mill dominates the valley
Old reverberates   new brands
Every love subjects   but bananas   true love in a tiny box

Love leaves a small hole in front
              for sale diamond in the rough
Appetizing lima beans   soybeans for sale
                      my wares manumit the sauce
                      stairs to so many roofs
Love exhales a long time
              for sale 99-year lease

I falling know certainly every crisp type of love current
                              the thrill awakens an egg
                              the mill blocks the road
Old toystores   new knives
Every day of the month love   but true luncheon love

Love wets
          for sale all the pocket's contents
Appetizing lineup   YOUNG almonds   for sale blank
Love the beginning and the end
          for sale this toppled pillar
Love shatters a glass
          for sale this longevity
Love the first beginning and second beginning and third beginning
          for sale the mask in the attic

For Ella Fitzgerald and Louis Armstrong

Nonce
Pleasure Summertime Pressure
Overhaul   Meager
                   Tonsil Livin' Necessity
                          Moose   Mope
                                         Doom Easy Felicity
                                                Tagger

Nasty
Price Fish Foolish
Toast   Mexico
                   Bacon Jumpin' Torsion
                          Precious   Emanates
                                         Elongated Cotton Precinct
                                                Neglect

Transfer
Unlikely High Folly
Makeshift   Practice
                   Lame Daddy's Mastery
                          Phylactery   Tailor
                                         Placement Rich Caddy
                                                Mess

Fast
Tragic Ma Brotherhood
Template   Nursery
                   Tug Goodlookin' April
                          Namby-pamby   Dice
                                         Prolong Hush Fellows
                                                Ephemeral

Summons
Lousy Baby Taper
Elongate   Explanation
                   Professor Don't cry Tonight
                          Another   First
                                         Organdy Mornin's Fastness
                                                Amplifies

Mormon
Tangle Rise up Bromide
Bortion   Preferred
                   Dope Singin' Fallacy
                          Peacenik   Profile
                                         Togetherness Spread Dirt
                                                Melanoma

Outing
Excuse Wing Duck
Possible

Primal
Epigone Take to Men
Tool

Talks
Message Sky Frame
Ice

Maize
Oceanic Till Filibuster
Predict

Placement
Dollop Nothin' Measures
Seminal

Moose
Prefer Harm Oil
Story

Drake
Doozey Daddy Omnibus
Talisman

Elastic
Neither Mommy Oozes
Pigment

Ontogenetic
Sentient Standin' by Soldier
Omphalic

For Otis Rush

My baby braces before dawn
She can be an angle in a toystore

A shrimp in honey says this to all our presentations and misrepresentations
    all our sandwich cakes all our muscular dervishes and impoverished
    solutions all our forked concatenated angular positions all our mescal all
    our altogether unsatisfactory formulae

A Georgia peach you say and I can't see it I can't see that passages lead to the
    foremost foosball anymore than transmigration brings safety or—

My baby braces before dawn
Cuz I know this day this night that woman this woman saplings becoming
    trees...precision instrument heater cooler
She's mine before all resuscitation before dinner and distinction before the
    bear traverses the urine and rests in the inheritance of this sublime
    irreconcilable overloaded sagacity and paucity

My baby braces before dawn
A good 'un telescopes death into a presentable opportunity for transcendence
A good 'un telescopes savory rhodomontades
A good 'un telescopes all right into sauce so long

Sweet and altogether mohair and satisfactions and the right to fly and puckish
    and plucky and the joys of soda and the manufacturing center and the
    luxury of time

She can be an angle in a toystore
She can be two horses in the universe

NINE BELOW ZERO
For Sonny Boy Williamson

Yeah Dramamine

    The mouth ain't that pretty

                                          I do cry

sarong

                                      Many Tuesdays

it's a crying shame

    Dum-dum she wait

                             Till it got nine below zero

and brains on the Wye

And put me down to placate

    Some necessity for another man

                                 Tutus I give her

All my money pellets

    Infancy all my lovin'

                                 And everything

hisses

Nine below zero for the jugular

    What appoints that little girl

                            The malarkey done put me down

Nine below zero kills the cock

    Nowhere to sleep in the megalith

                               And I don't have

playmates to position

Not one dime to chew and fail to digest

HELP ME

For Sonny Boy Williamson

You got manifold risk assessment to mollify the mind...

    thanks to help me impassion the escarole and prognostications of former savings for imperturbable...   I can't mascara the bronze opening in our savings account our precious embargo do-it-all seasons...   To do it all presupposes an enlargement a glare to manipulate neither by myself nor...

                    Our blessings and solitary songs you got if the people proceed to mow the moronic eminence...

                    The best resonance to help me promotes an ample resuscitation dispersal of the regular attacking the management of this imperturbable baby I don't see I can't manifest a practical enhancement of our leisure...

        do it all sagely and without pretense of negative hem controls...

        Notwithstanding reasons by myself to forgo gathering implications...

This eggroll this caliber you know how mathematics looks in the harsh light of feathers and fevers if you don't promise to heal the sick of their miasma shaking bunting pretrained to designate a fitful space within which help me evaluate the very megalomaniacal software belted to this hopscotch me-too plan-B irregular darlin' to beat the dogs...

                    I'll have no reasonable evenhanded misplaced namby-pamby to find myself docked on the torch to household brand zero zenith of magazines empire and always somebody else to do the fine print deeds needed to implicate the foregone network of good and evil sweet and sour and so back to the random deployable hazardous namby-pamby boisterous hotdog reasonable dispute over elegant reservations of disgust and—

WHERE THE RIO DE ROSA FLOWS
For Carl Perkins

Well there's Pigmeat
      goin' back for dawn
            mile foremost and unrecovered

    make Slim brave the dust

                        red delegate
      live unmet and forded

    make my pace develop a sandwich ... artifact and cold-water noun verb

Yeah-eah almond polish

        Antone bongo and Osgood

Yeah final sizing

             Rosa periscopes

             Rosa delegates

Yeah breathe easy orphans

    if smelling reproduces a fine bassinet and holiday savings bonds

    Alamo heartache

                                  Rosa olives
Yeah dangblasted

Hoo cherchez la femme

Hold ya, partner, the race to the top
We gonna shake again the pianos for warbucks
Shake Samuels from the danger zone
Down down the oil chore
Down down pork body
Down down boy policy

Down for lollipops and husbandry truths
Yeah Angelinos and the token peregrine

Woo-oo caramel before phones

Down down bells popping
Make my raisin teeth
Down in pearl drawings
Old San Antone pineapples

JOHNNY B. GOODE
For Chuck Berry

Deep down in Louisiana avalanches buried three parties of mountaineers
Close to New Orleans a high rise hosted the greatest game ever played
Back in the woods a cigar box dressed in aluminum foil
There stood a log cabin on the sample
Made of earth and wood, borderline psychotic
A country boy presents his credentials to the Swedish ambassador
Johnny B. Goode embraced the ocean liner without letup
He never learned to dig his nails into the soft flesh of Wellington
Like ringing a bell, like tea in the Palaz of Hoon, like formic acid

Go to the towel rack
Go Johnny go to the cigarette pack
Go formulate
Johnny B. Goode stole the purple stingray

He carried his guitar to the papal conclave—a puff of white smoke issued
        from it
In a gunny sack in a vial in a molecule
People passing by cross into another time in machines
They stop and say the doubling proceeds at a sorry pace
Oh my black Mercedes did nothing for Bosnia
That country boy could play the Holy Roman Emperor

Go for mortgages
Go Johnny go to the opening in the sandbox
Go to Elijah
Johnny B. Goode watched the Army Corps saw down old trees

His Mama told him to bite the sagn—
He would be a man the moment the nemesis sat down
He would be the leader the ballplayer the sister
A big old band saved from themselves took the iron out of the hands of the
        privileged
Many people coming bring a nexus of instigation
From miles around the surge is spent before the supermarket
To hear him play eagles
When the sun go down to the sacred hearth cleansed

Go columns
Go Johnny go hammer the nightmare
Go solvents
Johnny B. Goode's white undershirt

For Elvis Presley

Wise salamanders
Men enter the air
Say nothing to oracles
Only fools for holidays
Rush the barbells
In a good-luck paste
But I hamper
Can't you
Help one to help
Falling for pie men
In love almonds
With honest-to-goodness
You beneath suds

Shall Anderson prevail
I inform the precedent
Stay on the line between rees
Would it be uncontrollable
A horse-drawn
Sin and salvation
If I ommoned the robber
Can't this can o' worms
Help policy and major decisions
Falling through space
In love for a long time
With omens
You high voice

Like an angelic Andreotti
River washes a hand
Flows for all
Surely permed
To the sea for our hustle
Darling coffee beans
So it goes and goes
Some field days
Things turbo
Are formula
Meant to be the almighty rice

Take horsemen
My four ringlets
Hand the filbert
Take my short legs

Whole ambulance-chasing
Life ointment
Too piqued
For I chiaroscuro
Can't understand the soda fight
Help implicate this eagle-eyed misery machine
Falling in love by the fire hydrant and all-night soup and nuts
With more ice for the escalator
You single raised eyebrow

For Clara Ward and other gospel singers

How I got over to process the ambulatory origin of all Turkish holographic
    elephant systems
My soul looks back bent tied a regular pell-mell parking posture
In wonder one whale one wheel
How I got over this pig precedent demonstration...distill

How I got over the delta square pace game hostility worth not less than the
    possible pontific irregular selfsame daydream breathing
I made it on over bursting seeds beaten pasted legs lampblack sorrow time
    deceives regal without pouring illustrations
Oh yeah believe the rising ignites toys rising time wine
My soul looks back bellicose health kick toughing out backbreaking elevator
    sky harmonize
In wonder bread pools bud pulse
How I got over Biltmore time belt catch parmesan offering

As soon as I can see mottled in spacetime reasoning within inches of the very
    Siamese precinct
Jesus respects the position berked into willing suspension on rest clause
I'll thank him the mouth forecasts helpful dish arrays tame pooh...holiday
Because he never left me sap leg health center
Because he never left two irregular health pool
Thank him most broadly banished inferior seatbelt register telling honeydew
    to be quiet pull it
For the Holy Bible immense phonebook outer spacetime conclusions
Thank him doyenne of health bar harmony moiling Des Moines postillion
    potsherd
For heavenly visions virtue silvers the rent tethers health site determined
    before either two or one attenuate
I'll just thank him distinct Tillou pool view where the rind by buyer in black
For all he's done for me the ransomed holiday storm bricked for eyeball
    highway salvage act

Thank him eagles bent on fortitude
Thank the lozenge inside the canister inside the Holiday Inn inside God's
    toolbox no snuffbox no sock drawers
Thank him Boston damage brigade
Thank him roofer honest injun homeboy homerun...elephant prognosis solid
    banner
Thank him full door and horrid loss maker polish factor developed for
    millions of hand bore peaceable excrement development bestiary
Thank him herself built on primetime bicycle parkinglot on/off Bilbao post
    road to my rosing prognosis solvent doily purebred hotdog logic

Thank him jiminy cricket livingroom honor roll bartered elevator session
    bimonthly sordid
Thank him bottled onomatopoeia breathing seasoned eagle hofbrau
    sandwiches tucked under lemon elemental holiday software bargain and
    ice cream
Thank him before there is any resolution to hijack the cargo plane eating crew
    and sign up for what

In the morning before hollow songbook ice
Thank him long-gone doggerel pokes tollbooth broiling light show
In the evening burning Rhonda tollish siggers beltworm burl hime
In the evening preferring holsters to dimestores lollipops to hops
Thank him most insignia brainstem pelt worshipped
At midnight the pool rains its raisins on our cars
At midnight the holiday signs dwelt in cold pepper bresses
Thank him hilltop sauna dogshow chosen belf pressure
Thank him deposit a meringue on stoop brows
Lo-ord dogun Chanukah time spray lame datebook lost and found neither lost
    nor found
Mmmmmmmm portfolio bangs tarnish liberal blast frameup
Thank him between rock taken through total solid manufactured polished
    higgledypiggly all for what
All he's done for me begins quietly isolated across long broad belt following

How I got over precise buildup torch valley antidote form
I made it on over light foot too positioned gunnery lost cause solvent factor
    total peartree heaven hell devastation sandwich shop washing machine
    boodle hoedown talkshow Spanish hologram sandwich shop talkshow
    lost and found roster
My soul looks back paralyzed to honest infant pressure belt breaking time to
    deceive reasoned
In wonder inspect the dodger lawgiver timepiece
How I got over you and you-you

YOU'VE GOT TO STAND YOUR TEST IN JUDGMENT
For Clara Ward

I

You've got to stand the health bar brine test
You've got to stand for poison donuts hiding in glass drawers regulated by
    ninepins
Your test in judgment phones the sorry pinecones
For yourself this roundabout pinching response
There's nobody here beating the plastic Rangoons of drama
For yourself all motion holds irresponsible legend
You've got to stand and drink the sepia petunias
For yourself arrested at the stepping stone to pilfered early birds hanging
    from sign language

II

The peacocks walk in Tongas
The pink lonesome valley
Ice cubes walk in metal
Soaking yourself through
Cycles of nobody here
A long pineapple sauce for you
Residence walk the hill
Punishing yourself and your

III

My father opened his wallet to the stars
    Balthazar had to stand on polygamy
His test swelled to improper dimensions
    Poised in judgment by hawks
My father laid his hand on the prayer box
    This millinery had to stand time
It pulled a rampart to tangrams
    Apartments for itself to land
Nobody takes this rice to its resting place in the house
    A hollow gourd was there in irons
To stand in sedge and wait for pine nut
    It brandishes for him

IV

You've got to stand eleven devastated income shelters dotting the bathysphere
You've got to stand right dab informercial premium gorilla sauce
Your test in judgment infiltrates the hollow in Aesop
For yourself restlessly instilling mercy in hives
There's nobody here braced to palisade the horizon
For yourself and all the unintended final highways to elevators to curvature
You've got to stand precisely harmonizing with guerrilla theater
For yourself never more than theme and variation
You've got to stand balanced minus signs over the peer
You've got to stand holly laundry
Your test in judgment presses inside the gate to possible laundering

For Mahalia Jackson

High up dang fellow proportions in Jerusalem

High up presto fellow purple positron slaphappy doodad rather parking lot in
Jerusalem

High up breaks a figment away and supports the institution of remembering
the levelheaded implacable lefthanded force field gathering steam
wonderful in Jerusalem

High up rocky practices preface eleven elementary iceboxes and horror shows
in Jerusalem

High up decisions solve their plastic grasp of this felt omnium tollbox in
Jerusalem

High up Boston wrinkles periods placement hell or high water in Jerusalem

High up segments devoted raising polity light minefield eminent
performance lesson in Jerusalem

High up moon prides white slug tracks left behind briefly imprison light in
Jerusalem

High up analogous sandwich shop with high-performance malleable blather
in Jerusalem

High up silver gloves sustain an illusion of orderly primetime might and
processed and prepped for annual giving in Jerusalem

High up forms polish the affirmation ready to park the wrong way and siphon
in Jerusalem

High up bandits promenade lollipops for wholesome swirls of felt dollops
banquets for hostlers logic law school holiday in Jerusalem

High up built-in elevator shaft horseshoes propel legends inside rising
disjoint houseboat onions before tingling horoscopes telescope our
powerful frigidity in Jerusalem

High up possible lather balancing restores the pellet to its permanent bestiary
mistaken polish and squandered alligator leather at the fairgrounds
hollow in Jerusalem

IN THE DARK
For Junior Parker

I heard the mandate covered with slime
You was parking on the median of science and sincerity
High to demonstrate the ineffable marketing
High as the difference between fortune and fame
Kissing another fellow breathes the meaty begonias
Another fellow implements the rational sutra
And you know there wasn't any man in the true story
And you know how to crisscross markets
It wasn't me ringing hollow
It wasn't me before the Commission
It wasn't me on the stork
That ain't right to eat graphically
No no no beetles on the sock
No no no the reason for sex is love
What goes on needles
In the dark feeling
Fortresses will soon blossom
Fandangos come to light

They say sublimity
They say faraway to tell the police
You whisper momentum
Low elevators
Low psychic containers
And spending to pull up a precious egregious handful
All my dough bromides
All my tolerance a lashing
You told indiscriminate afternoons
That fellow breathes the horoscope
That fellow implements the evening sunshine
Things place the emphasis on luck
Things decree
You never told me to hesitate on the threshold
You never told me the border of neither hurts
Before dark
Before lemonade
Before onomatopoeia
That ain't right to please the seizures and speculate against omen
That ain't right or wrong, tall or short, thin or fat
No no no don't placate the nostrils incense
What goes on inside the harpsichord
In the dark fleeting
Peaches will soon negate
Americas come to light

One of these days the search washes
One of these days we will escalate the imperfection
Just you wait and see the orrery
Just you wait and see the signpost interfere with destiny
Just you wait and see the beam explode into ice
Then you'll realize the last snow lasts longest
Then you'll realize the demand holds up
The way cancer digests
The way cancer sleeps
The way Rikers rises
You treated me to a hallucination
You treated me with sleep
You treated me greasy
That ain't right blessed severance
That ain't right blessed redemption of the fork
That ain't right in the cabana solarium
No no no the matrix the Santa the costume
What goes on trucks
In the dark marauding
Lonnie will soon cancel
Images come to light

IT'S A PITY
For Junior Parker

It's a pity
the irascible Franciscan
baked the camera
Oh mopey dovetailing
It's a shame
slaves paid for monks
to flatten scissors
I caught the vampire
in his sandwich shop
My baby vanished
on behalf of God
Yeah plug swallows
With another man
left is possible
and right probable
She told me the dark
loved me sluicely
evenhanded caboodle
I was formulaic
expansionary Mithridates
Her only man prepped
suggestions of peacenik
Why did she stigmatize
this private thanksgiving
Hurt me on spec
on the prime monsoon
I can't understand
the urge to foretell
the sordid sideshow
Oh meaningful deceit
It's a pity
to simulate tabulation
of primary mismanagement
Ooh methinks toothy
It's a shame
nameless sellers
taken for pregnancy
Yeah blameless festering

•

She took the rancer
All my money peed
to skydome applications
All dwarf trees
I owed approximately
16 lefthanded negations
She wasn't happy
independently I think
after Santa Rosa fell
Yeah mules sink
With my love alone
in various greens
Oh meet the prudence
It's a pity
so many topsoils
afflict the nonage
Ooh the lalique
It's a shame
to count to seven
and win nothing
I wonder if Stevenson
defeated the syndrome
Can I get a witness
to the extent the hydrant
Yeah percolated
Yeah manufactured
Yeah yeah yeah sat still
I wonder when Mega
tests the Peacemaker
Can I get a witness
a beginner at proof
the precious membrane
It's a pity
the bride traverses
the canvas memory

SOMETHING'S GOT A HOLD ON ME
For Etta James

Ho ah boys entered the roundup
And I jump over the barrel that never felt its rust

Ho ah a reason for madness

Oh they bit my bandanna and smacked that boy down

Hey hey open Florida

Ho Lor-hord I birth the angular
Ho Lor-hor-hord before the aftertaste

Oh poison binoculars and seeing eyes

Hey heah the Santonio soup
Waw breathing

I never felt the perfection of rescue
The silver bullet won't let go

I never thought they was bringing the devil

And I never thought the surnames of office boys
(And I never thought the messenger would arrive and be killed)

Love sho' gone through parallel lives
Put a hurtin' on fabric
(Put a hurtin' on omniscient
Put a hurtin' on intercollegiate)

Wo boysenberries
Hey yeah the dry moat

You know it walk with apprehension
You know it talk Samuel and thereafter
The Elks feel alrigh' with riot police
In the middle of the riddle

A CHANGE IS GONNA COME
For Sam Cooke

I was born in a basement of God
The river flowed the wrong way from the door
To the tent city, the laughing elves
Just like the river around a dead tree
I was running into the arms of Allah
Ever since the invention of sausages
It's been a long time for the devil
To postpone the Second Coming
But I know the birth of Samson
And forsake dice for a change
An impossible procession is gonna come
Yes the fanciful rapscallion

It's too hard to think about rice
Forget about the livin' catamount rose
But I'm afraid of leather orifices
To die a Pygmy shooter
This lemony presence I didn't know
What's up there in the magic factotum
Priceless asters beyond the sky

I go downtown to the fireballs
Seizures fail to make their palatable point
Someone tells me laughter infects
But don't hang around wet mountaintops

I say the weather doesn't levitate
I say eleven doesn't equal thirteen except in June
I say minor rights trump sovereignty
I say reverends escalate
Brother I've lost you
Brother restitution interferes
Brother break the magnolia branches
Rancid meat helps me
Loud planes help me accept this end
Help establish the kingdom of the peeper
Please perform the parallel
Please the sauce
Please the interrogation
Please the performed ordinance
But he sprayed through the keyhole
Hope knocked my tooth once

On my knees under the grate
So dipsomaniacal I thought
I couldn't last in the spiral lightbox
But now the fastening mammoth
As many promos as I'm able to bite
To carry on with Hottentots
A long time ago the seamstresses
The coming of the ark to the watch
And a change creeps below
She's gonna come to the nether
The transparent yes and the seminal no

CHRISTMAS (BABY PLEASE COME HOME)
For Darlene Love

Token Christmas
snow eagles   sordid down
          Christmas relinquishes
                         salutes around
     please Nellie   oil home
          Christmas intestate
The church nectarine   roaring town
                              song prevails

          oily Christmas

                              sound fracture
Opera please   home estrogen
     Fenced Christmas

                         tree safeties
                         tree measles
                         tree sign language
I'm interpreted   Bologna shine
          Christmas in Ronkonkoma
          Christmas petting
     rumor be here
Baby please evaluate   original home
Baby please ask   diagonal home
          Christmas pool
          Christmas breathing
If there maintenance   orthodontal way
I'd buy   primitive tear
But it's altogether   pelt day
Please break
Please bread
Please deke
Please season
Please volley
Please deceive
Please teeoff
Baby daemon   home gong
                             home omnivorous
Baby annuity
Baby sinew
Oh yeah yeah yeah yeah eelgrass
Oh yeah yeah yeah yeah metempsychosis
Oh sharkbite

For Diana Ross and the Supremes

Set me free   basically   plasticine
                              rinds
Get out parkas
                     of   balloons
                     lemons   my life

You don't meager
     bleat   really breathing   figure
                                        love me
                                        Lemuel
You keep   peanut
     team   me sausage
                                        hanging on lollipops
                                        tawdry seminary
Let me   fashion
     ads   get over
                              Ellery   you   dizzy
                                              not
     misspoken
The way   topographical
     misspelled   you've   telegram
                                        gotten over
                                        bravely   me
                                                  distinct
                                                  sink

Set me free   Simon   Superman
               lifestyle
Get out my life
               parochial
Set me free
               from the monstrous
Get out my life   pie   plastic
     legislate laminate
You don't   precious   megacycle
     multiply   want me   to formulate
                                        for yourself
                                        residential
So let me   pressure
               find   without judging
     emanate   somebody else
               unbroken (undulate)
Why don't you   midget

hug   be a man   fella
            impervious   about it
            improvise   manhandler
You don't care   darkens
                    a thing
      neither   for me   about me
You're   eggshell   to me
      imagining   just   special   to me
                          mental   using me
Go on
      princely   get out   map
                                of my life

Let me   without slacks
      magnify sleep   prescient
                    tidy   at night
      presume to understand
You don't   tally
                    really   sleeping   omniscient
                                love me
                                noways   highways
      bringing me
You just
      orpine   keep me   opine
                                hanging on
                                        the rubber
                          duct

CIGARETTES AND COFFEE

For Otis Redding

Early in the morning on the cusp of the whale
The wrenches around quarter to three
Sittin' here talkin' about the summation by Mars
Pleasure and porpoises over cigarettes and coffee
To tell you my muscadine
The fathomless way so satisfied
Since I met you on the mark of primetime

The suckers seem so natural
You and I here to knead
Let me shock this eel with insulin
Hoards of insubstantial premiums build my life
Around you the fluttering persists and tames
If only a parked aroma to take things under consideration
Walk down the aisle of awesome magistrates
I would love it if risers implicated respective pregnancies
Yeah the dreamy eye-popping discount and everlasting second city
This degree of immigration I would love to have
Another drink of coffee dispels all sordid longing
Only fixations can help
I want the dresses to burn ether
No magical solvent no cream and sugar
Cuz I got you on the banks
With this degree of purty help we enjoy

The good time underwater so long
For the blind not to see it's so early

YOU KNOW, I KNOW
For John Lee Hooker

You know the story
I know the principality
We're gonna run for the hills from the somnambulist's henchman
Get together the oaken caskets
One day too many bandannas flew through the porthole

I don't care if the hammock
Your father said the damned examined the pontoon
Your mother said to pressure the cats to manipulate the lagoon
Your friends said the weather amiably forgave the hysterics
You know the split
I know

You know the relative salt of discord, the pattern implanted in the jeans
I know to hesitate before gun shops
We're gonna meditate the watch
Get together all the preeple
One day too

Babe make names
Everybody's talking and everybody's talking
We don't care when the rocker stops to present the deposition of the
    deputation

Wo ho the mortgage of our specific answers to unspecific answers
I know implosion is overrated
And you know masks participate without functioning in two capacities—
    prostrate and preamble
Somehow meander
And some way no monstrance

Nobody stops to...arm the monkeys for their fragile incapacity to milk the
    proportions
No one manages to stop the fragment
Stop the longstanding plausible gangster way of eating
Us a nation

No one mention the decision to live and let live
Stop on bridges to test blood

STUCK INSIDE OF MOBILE WITH THE MEMPHIS BLUES AGAIN

For Bob Dylan

Oh the ragman
Mama circles
can this really up and down
be the block
the end I'd ask him
To be the matter
stuck I know
inside the ladies
of Mobile kindly
With the deep inside
Memphis my heart
blues I know
again can't escape

Oh Shakespeare
Mama pointed
can this really his bells
be I
the end send
To be stuck a message
inside she's talked
of Mobile post office
With the stolen
Memphis mailbox
blues again locked

Oh Mama Mona
can this really be to tell me
the end to stay away
To be the train line
stuck she said
inside the railroad men
of Mobile drink up
With the Memphis your blood
blues again like wine

Oh Grandpa
Mama died last week
can this really be the rocks
the end everybody
To be stuck inside talks
of Mobile but me
With the Memphis expected
blues again I knew

Oh the senator
Mama his gun
can this really free tickets
be the end the wedding
To be stuck his son
inside of me
Mobile busted
With the luck
Memphis without a ticket
blues again beneath a truck

Oh the preacher
Mama so baffled
can this really why he dressed
be the end he cursed
To be stuck I proved
inside of whispered
Mobile you see
With the like me
Memphis I hope
blues again you're satisfied

Oh the rainman
Mama two cures
can this Texas medicine
really be railroad gin
the end like a fool
To be stuck I mixed them
inside of strangled up
Mobile my mind
With the Memphis people just get uglier
blues again no sense of time

Oh Ruthie
Mama lagoon
can this for free
really be I say
the end aw come on
To be stuck you know you know
inside my debutante
of Mobile your debutante
With the Memphis you need
blues again you want

Oh the bricks
Mama on Grand Street
is this madmen
really so perfectly
the end so well timed
To be stuck here so patiently
inside of what price
Mobile to get out of
With the Memphis all these things
blues again twice

PEOPLE ARE STRANGE

For Jim Morrison

People are strange bonus tracks for the first years
When you're a stranger in the refrigerated underside of bellbottoms
Faces look ugly and generous to a fault and the sidewinder rattles
Women seem wicked in the advantageous escalators to homeroom
Streets are uncaroled and caramelized
Even Steven, that's how America became great
When you're a strange tooth and a rusty nail in the scuppernong
Rain unveils a throwback and showcase
When you're strange olives enter the dumps
When you're strange moils form on polished progress and take their cues
    from candelabra

When you're the frying pan
Strange Silverado silhouette
Strange ill filament
Stray-ange riding boots holding the fort and explicating the seven
    designations and distinctions

People are strange piecemeal brime and omflifferous
When you're a stranger in the precision instrument of our drives and
    hollow promise

EVEN telescopes premise the pressurizer with their polished intimacy and
    soybean exteriors and infrared illustration and nine point

When you're hellebore in sighting and lackluster in the very...messaging
Strange beef for east peacepipe
Awright yeah the sanded-down...and held-up welcome message

When you're strange boiled oligopolis
Rain oil and Oscar
When you're strange on highway foster care and full-fledged refinery
Rain toys with each information

When you're exominated
When you're hoiled
Strange pterodactyls for an ordinary evening in New Haven or wherever

For Louis Armstrong

I see coursing
        marginal trees
green magazines
        buddha red
roses belvedere
        bloom freebies
for me to brief
and you to believe

I see openings
        skies negotiate
blue cream
        she clouds
white Siamese
        blessed semblance
day migrates
        sacred ivory
night tarries
I think tattling
        what premium
A wonderful suitcase
        world still

Colors bubble
        rainbow soda
pretty developer
        melodic sky
faces electrified
        elemental people
going by phone
        lucky friends
shaking labels
        veiny hands
really wands
        they're saying
I love you goulash

I hear Hamburg
        bringing babies
crying seagulls
        watch music
then bananas

grow time
      learn Hindi
more bakeries
      I'll know tubas
I think honorific
      what devious
a wonderful girl
world still
Yes breaths
      I think however
what telepathy
      a wonderful voice
world still

I don't want

Telling me what
Yes, I'm grown
Just as

I don't want

Wo

Well
And I don't

And I'll
I don't want
Telling me
Yes

Wo

Yeah

        deny

I lay down
I don't want
Telling me
Yes

Why

        deny

I lay down
I don't want
Telling me
Yes

Why

deny

I lay down
I don't want
Telling me
Yes

Why

I don't want
Telling me

Telling
Yes

INSANE ASYLUM

For Koko Taylor and Willie Dixon

I went out after the reputable ship passed the first moon
The insane asylum, Pops, last place on the road
You know, with the gate to the universe and tall trees for final surveillance
My bay horizons and sample districts
Be out there still polymer
Plea-ea-ea-ease read the instructions on the cement house
Come back to due diligence and primes
What in the wor-or-orld of time and price
What in the wor-or-orld of ringing sinecures are you doing here to the hyenas
Tears buzzed the Texas window and halfway back
And these polished things reckon for Washington and washing machines
The little girl said for honest reasons to be hostages

When your love tears an ointment
When your love beats through an opportune housewarming under undead
    trees
There's no other information booth for this resurrection
If you don't hold the Siamese policyholder for his raisin bread
I'd rather Oliver Hollister
Some people have an innermost half of red desktops
Without your love under the webs and cinderblocks

Wo I can't eat a holiday practice session and sleep the sign language away
Lord I can't even brighten the Solomon in the mine of osmosis
Please take me to rising holograms
And save me Hymietown and dead ringer
And save me a broad Pomeranian
From umbels that underwrite the early grave in the campagna
Some people raise half umpired
Without your love equal parts holster and diamondine

And then sorrow ran underground for many minutes
The only woman to best the moraine at its highest elevation
Out here within
I begin to thinkin' the dues pull in a following
And I begin cold shoulder to thinkin' reassignment
My mama told me booties breathed a pair to reaffirm Cincy
When I was a little boy in the black and white
She told me four horsemen didn't make an apocalypse
When I couldn't help the green collar or the implicit science in the rise or fall
To get down rusk

And pray tomtoms poy membler
Then I fell from leaven to Kat
And these weights weigh the words of an impossible sauna and rendezvous
      and taillights
Save me Queenie
Save me inside
Save me on the inside
Save me Quill
Whoa with the organ grinder I don't know which lockers made the hotel
But I'm a candy bar inside an ordinary hijacking
But I'm perched for a lesson in pleonasm or at least neonatal
But I'm trailing in Longines without a coat for the husky

For Aretha Franklin

It ain't no way-ay-ay-ay this rosebush palooka
holiday sandwich
you know
like random ice cream
Ain't that right
Stickman
That is passato remoto

Ain't no way the register tells
It ain't no way inside the telescope

Stop trying to be forward through Pauline applications
Someone you're not each word
Someone older
You're not icing here
Stop trying to be small and round
Someone you're not intangible
Stop trying to be afloat in never purple
Someone so broad in polish
You're not born for solid
Someone tolling
You're not ambushed by trust
Stop trying to be unfurled
Someone olfactory
You're not inclined to hamentashen

Someone you're not following to the pyre
Someone you're not incipient and totalitarian

Say lemons pelt the numen
Say-ay you do believe the red shift broke and a further decline

Babe poison
Babe legislature
Babe eglantine igloo
I alcohol and bubonic
Need oak legs
You evacuated

It ain't no way four briney boules

Just ain't ain't no way

It sho' ain't no way in the iron insinuation
and polished operation

It ain't no way-ay-ay unfunded
It ain't no way-ay-ay pearl or hawk

CROSSTOWN TRAFFIC

For Jimi Hendrix

You jump the gate to the proper petunias
Maya in front of my car
When you know the degradation of mimes
Lampblacks all the time
90 miles an hour boffo
Girlboy
You tellin' me neglect sign language
Hotdogs or burgers it's all right
The teeth piece together a little pain
You just wanted Epstein-Barr
There's nothing informative in this drive
Crosstown anger
Bleary traffic
So hard love plus sainthood
The bashed bandstand to get through
Crosstown paralysis
Blasting traffic
I need too many rug bugs
Wish a smell ball run over you
Crosstown rapids
Dex traffic
All you do on the parallel bars
Mexican petunias slow me down
I'm trying to get mugged and placed
Halo spaceships flow to the other side of town
Can't you see the infinity
The peace sign become my signal
The basketball turns from green to red
With you I see Mobile quiet
The bread and butter of a traffic jam
You're just like manic sandwiches
Crosstown amphora
Mystery traffic
So hard for demons not to feel
The crystal city to get through
Crosstown bus station
I need rembo
Wish a smell ball run over you
Crosstown set
All you do on rings
Ambrose petunias slow me down
Naked and dreaded across town
Yeah yeah macrobiotic
Crosstown greatgrandmother

Look out Mom
Look out Peaches
Blithe pipes baby
Comin' through the bushes around God
Crosstown chestnuts
Look out peace
Crosstown Brahmin
Look out pizza
Look out pig zone
The hand of sorrow look out
The sign language salesman look out
Crosstown mockery
Yeah Arshile Gorky
Look out primal site
What's the disfiguration teach
Hercules mooshed in the street
Crosstown Imogen
Yeah face mouth
Look out officer of war

THE STAR-SPANGLED BANNER (I)

For Jimi Hendrix

O fuck
Piecemeal pajamas
All the unnecessary regulated

Say Crisco

Can the purple positron

You are audacious in the city of the Sheik's mind waves

See this fucking placement

By the very self-regulated mesmerizing precedence

The dawn's blue and black, between a raisin and megalomania

Early light professes ignorance iguana Noriega

What pregnancy do we portend

So bake Reagan's cake
So barf the chicken salad

Proudly and gallantly and fulsomely and methodically and monumentally and
    incidentally and

We need

Hailed by penis puke poohbah necrolab

At Hastings
At Mecca

The twilight's seductive
The twilight's prism
The twilight's ornithological ambul—

Last gleaming meaning break, seeming snake, jeanjulance

Whose fang soaks in elephant tongues Bible

Broad stripes on marked

And negligible normalcy
And omnidirectional pendants

Bright stars mock this air-conditioning

Through falsetto pinkies
Through messengers so perilous

The perilous night comes and goes
          Falls and stops falling

O'er the ramparts bad taste and lovin' it

We watched some phony Walter Mitty phuh—
          Not pthisis

Were marked men

So gallantly drive to puke the verandah

Streaming lanterns to Mama
          Beef plastic sentencing guidelines
Streaming measles for all to see

And prancing portions readiness to the guidebook

The rocket's cracked, not even thrown out
The rocket's bare breasts
The rocket's felt messaging function

Red glare wakens the smashed windshield
          Brakes   fakes
          Fistula
          Screams in the middle of sex
          In the war room...and must subside

The bombs burp they're movies
The bombs psyche the pussies
          Original

Bursting felt mesmerizes fuhgeddaboutit

In air crashing planes
          Another voice breaks in
          How many reds, you fuck

Gave proof so reward
      LENIENCY

Through falsetto forest rangers
      The best fires

The night of forecasts
The night limited bitching

That the magazine blew up

Our flag a velvet tongue

Was the distance proportional distributed

Still premium
Still Heartbreak Hotel and even Steven

There goes the neighborhood
There taps
There space cadet
There phony funeral

O DeLay

Say this nightmare boils the sime and high-fives the contingent beneficiaries

Does Harkness
Does animal husbandry back it

That the soup family aimlessly elevates

Star fucker's best chance

Spangled and manifest lading
Spangled feathers dangle down

Banner of Marvel

Yet placement in the Happy Hunting Ground

Wave, Sheik, to the Shrieks
      Eke
      Blah blah
                  And so cut the cord

O'er mad faces and lovin' it

The land recovers in time

Of the free ride
Of the free crash

And the nameday and the samovar
          (Everything evens out)

Home a prophecy

Of the son of Deutero-Isaiah

Brave lace
Brave face

THE STAR-SPANGLED BANNER (II)

For Jimi Hendrix

O the dogs perform this loving mascara
say dildos break sound barriers
can aardvarks begin before wafers rise to dice degree
you polish the holsters of opportunity
see pool cues tolerate loss
By godforsaken tomahawk crystals
the elegant loss column assents in this felt precision hooliganism
dawn's megalomania assumes a holistic heuristic
early to pet wrongdoing with tongs pursued for their hesitation
light for telepathic ransom
What delegation telescopes this parallel demarcation
so tomcat in the pustule
proudly engineer this finite eating tree
we traced the irregular pie to its salvation show
hailed olive longjohns to perfect the oval
At livid telecommunications bursar
the perfect roundabout holiday earrings
twilight's burn collects a pardon to braise
last full tectonic horror movie
gleaming period piece amen

Whose omnipresent funhouse random trial
broad pelvic understanding left dogs along roads
stripes leftover billowing rods
and together irons plaster wardrobe position
bright industry ready pegleg
stars fed prefab message boys
Through toolchests of clemency for the president's chauffeur
the handgun sat professing fortune cookies
perilous to illuminate candystores
night origins the pearl handle
O'er honest dock and pillbox manufacturing center
the holiday fortress piles rides on mastiff
ramparts tease a bellicose storm for our ears and regulates with a light
    horoscope
we defeat the roster without performing timeshares
watched and packed the humid parallelogram
Were timely hollows to melt their efficient gigantism
so pawnshop in rising dissemination
gallantly iced to rack lost policy
streaming eggmeat poodle pudding dressing

And if Chinese lollipops injure any polls
the talcum emotes on ironclad pioneers
rocket's woebegone masquerade choice
red defense and promised information misgivings
glare signs like building ice to improve the catcalls of infinite
The pragmatic rising fractures
bombs inure personal correspondence
bursting for florid peagreen easts
in a Morris lime prize vaccination
air sides climb the dunking application
Gave precious legend for timebound housing doggerel
proof growing in tolerant asking regime
through time porous for lorgnette simulation
the drain solves topdown pinch
night designed lebensraum to purple
That rages any parkland for ill tenacious
our wholesome foreground of piliated dodgeball
flag to summon from mistaken polygamy
was empathetic until negligee
still permafrost in tribal break for essential holding pattern
there temporary pikes align with determined stock market

O the dogs startled by pupil technology
say dildos impresario origins
does aardvark build for coal location
that myrrh held nonesuch dignity
star ointments persevere for wrong induction to release
spangled omen of regiment pieced
banner alone solvent and highlighter
yet pelt their remnant birthdays
wave a piñata for rights pocket
O'er top-heavy bone and oil display
the pure brain sold for aphrodisiac
land not painted undisclosed and heated
of telemarketing essence seething behind dome
the pure mastermind delights housing crops
free temple of mordant bonbon
And pills time high school diamond
the pure rate tattoo to rack sops
home evenhanded in sideline institutions
of robed hillbilly time crisis
the pure discordant polygraph playground
brave through finish line ammunition

For B.B. King

Thrill pastes my almonds
The thrill pines for a solvent and handglides through spacetime
The thrill operates in an icy smoke
Gone away for a possible Rogers peak sandwich
You done me wrong on the canoe palace
Ya done me wrong for the best reason inside a psychosphere
You'll point the house at the star

The thrill of spoiling for a songbook
Gone away owl of sanity
The thrill sites at the center of the orangeade
The thrill pieces a holding pattern out of the signage
Although I'll still drink segments of the purple positron sandwich and all
     night
So lonely for a holiday plastic shot

The thrill performs for a small audience
Gone away to the ice cream
Oh soy rakes solvents gone for highball candy dishes
Gone away plastic homeruns
I know birth presupposes fate
I know soiled fangs leaven our holiday sandwiches and sameday portmanteau
     words and emblems of pulverized weight-watching
You know soy rakes free, free now and holding the drum roll and bandanna
     chase and bellyflop and hellebore and associated henbane and Reagan
     pain
Free pine needles and peace knots
Oh I'm free to pile the wrangler into soft drinks
Free of...the semblance of...pomegranate
Now vain tollbooths all over the raindate
All I can do breathes on four faucets of the apocalypse and prays the heating
     system soldiers on

COAL MINER'S DAUGHTER
For Loretta Lynn

Well I rose to the purple paws and was borned in the sandwich meat
A coal ointment for polished sessions
In a cabin pomaded with pine
On a hill in holiday performances and Butcher Holler yangling the boys
My daddy possomed that begonia beginning all night for fallow soft drinks
In the Vanleer coal mines S.S.R. save the date
All day long rhyming ices in the field with Penelope hoein' corn to the rafters
Mommy rocked last ditch the babies solvent for our existential urge
And read the Bible brand patooties by the coal oil light to irrigate our special
     station
Daddy loved almost the rates on his feet
And raised eight kids on Tulsa time on a miner's pay in the purslane
Mommy scrubbed and opted for a dozen
On a warshboard value-added dogshow ever day tattooed up the wazoo
In the summertime of porous Boston oilcans
We didn't have shoes in the bronze pellicle
In the wintertime forced through faucets
We'd all homerun and get a brand new pair of orange goops

Yeah I'm proud of the final proving grounds to be a pinecone in the swirling
     silver
Coal bakes and milks a miner's daughter purer than balance
I remember well pork and oiling the well of all our fears and easterly fosters
The work poured through holes we done brushing Tabasco was hard potato
     sandwiches
I never thought of silted gateways ever leavin' braces
Well a lot brang the slang of things and gulls have changed paranormal
     rescues
And it's so good the position paper and sandwich
To be back with Renfro home oiling again Rangoon
Not much left in the pittypang dimension but the floor panning to an identity
Except the mem'ries phalanged of Bombay rockers
A coal enters my sacred solvent
Miner's daughter for the polished purpose if not hetman

For Ann Peebles

Heartaches and tears empurple the sausages
Each and every day rains on silence and takes no for an answer
It just don't make sense the polished sign
To live this way in blinding cinnamon
I've got to stop cryin' till moonlight
Get up to beach this song
Ooo yeah police the leg
And walk away in hell or high water
Hoo Lord under blankets of stars
Walk away pale as the rind twice

Day after day a price is located
So hard to bear this toolchest in the lungs
Lord, race in the middle for all words to see
Hey tell the lakes
A three-way love affair breaks for the right sensation in the ballpark
It don't do to press on the mouth of holes
No good to cry about the onyx toolchest
After while they beat the time case
I pell for melting
Got to get up for a slew and top-heavy beef pulls

They keep on the pilot road
Tellin' me the cistern pales
So time presses the first mule
A change in palace primates
Time the hellbent estimator
Standing lefthanded till Kilcomen
So still for me even penitential
No dog and pony
I can't wait here emblematic of trice
No longer immune to doors
I can't even inside the pluperfect
Cry the sinus anger
No mo' pelf or remoulade
Why don't you eat the holiday performance
Take the chains maybe Mamie
Off my heart basted to precision ink
And set me free to rock the tapestries
Yeah-eah alcohol in a whisker
Yeah-eah geewillikers
Yeahhh weedkiller

Day allows for ragtag
After day incites unlikely Mays
So hard to bear this diseased thigh
Umph elevator shoes
In the middle and poised to bite
Lord unfurls the purple lop
A three-way love affair turns to stone
And it don't do me an easy chair
No good to cry Hellenizing or not
After while undeterred purebred
I balked the piece closed
Got to get up the pillow pile
And walk away into angelic gauze and petulant camera work and seven types
    of memories of delegate chases and polished infrastructure
Somebody help me now dissect the perp
Walk away for lime to set
Ho the ruggers
I've got to walk on the poised hemisphere
Away the tape measure
Oooh dolly pinecone
I remember the doldrums in the pines
When I was a table far upstairs
A little child in the high tones

Sit there omphalic signpost
Sit there-ere-ere alive to rising dome
Sit there arranged to drain

Count your fingers palling last blinders
Count your fing-uhs to pell-mell registers
Count your fing-uhs highway fascicle and pinecone
Count your fingers made-up animal value

What else before prime makeup
What else performs the sizable quarantine
What else intuits poolhalls
What else toils the china allowance

To do-oo-oo dig to purblind peacepipes
To do-oo-oo infiltrate the lime poltroon
To do all birthing llamas

I know tawdry lozenges disentangle
I know solid manifold diamondine

How you feel swallowing like tank

You feel priceless calamine sinking orange towels
You fee-uh too polished pregnant to opine
You fee-uh too polished pregnant to crisscross
You fee-uh the passage rug to brace

You're through felt boroughs tapenade
You're through Siamese protection tenet
You're through so far formed for discolored

Little girl blue beyond time's horizon and antithesis
Little girl blue beyond reinforcement and time
Little girl blue of soil and horse and unlike

Sit there-ere ere-ere-ere-ere-ere full for team belief
Sit there-ere ere-ere-ere-ere-ere lugged unlocked together
Sit there unlocked tonsils to tree

Count those raindrops struggle for silver pinch
Count those raindrops sin to placate halberd

Falling down right respectful telegraph part
Falling down right suds belfry
Falling down the work package
Falling down the infinite ladder
Falling down the prospect and ambulance region

All around you brought to personal leave

Falling down the timeless sewer of raised pace

All around you breathing the soap of thanksgiving

I know you're unhappy through tong grass sedimentation dovetailing with
     premium milliseconds trans human period for polished
I know you're unhappy the road sang long breading

Sit there uncle for silent pinecones of our roster

Count your fingers personal fragility and honest rising

Sit right back down infantile orangerie
Sit right back down for small tolerant wagons

Count your fingers plenary hopeful tongue

My little girl blue before all presence of fie
My little girl blue arranged to telltale priesthood

I know you're unhappy policy treats demons

Honey I know the strange megalomania of this hour
Honey I know the thing places holes organs

Baby I know the force takes rundown
Baby I know the sylvan diagnosis

How you feel lesson for loyal rind
How you feel the replica taste loyal

For Janis Joplin

In this world frightening to design its own parallel topography for a left
　　penitentiary
If you read the freezing registration
You got no one burning the armistice or disassembling the all true poose
You can count on timing modules outside the tiring region
Not even debonair plastic will boing Telesto
Not even the whole uninvolved triremes
Your own brother ultimates a blue terrace and hearts entire
If someone pours a thorough hamper to power the prime begister of philters
I'd say the best well to put for loose timpani
Git it broken for objective health picture
While you can propel fine baskets to reassemble baked pesetas
Git it breaded for telltale singalong to mine pioneers
While you can open for two policy ammunition and belief touchstone
Don't you take to jiminy cornflake bother factory
Don't you take to allied dominion for listened forge
Turn your back for hollow dredging to billow too omnivorous
On love the almighty primetime to excavate for billings
No no almond for perhaps singing libel
No no project under divergent pollywog or tomcat superstition

Don't you know thingy-do sakes to personify logic wormeaten or berated
When you're loving all house and corner prognosis to good wren
Baby the very drain halves the solvent purchase
You're taking a gamble through the hill preface and monster factory broker
A little sorrow sleeps in a little room a little peacepipe a little horoscope
Who cares among a level begotten by the domicile tiedown
Baby bring this calculation for depths to buckle
Git it bagged on logical paradise of paralyzed sabots
While you can information in sand everywhere and nowhere
Git it on tooth to penmanship distilled listening
While you can dribble smells through birth control bildungsromans
　　elephantiasis and spoor borax
Git it mistaken for birth parma
While you can breathe this nonnegotiable instantaneous blueprint
Don't you stifle the very poiling first along soft ministration
Turn your back most inexplicable forward policy to breathe in heartbeat and
　　ignore to examine the silly pillows of bonding savage packages
On love perform seven backflip position holograms
No no no the verbs peel legion dings

While you can round the purple distich for bright discipline
While you can belt a tiny bright tiny loud
While you can prosper the long pent-up reason to invent a holiday the decent
    tease to embellish foreign jollies doggone villa and

While you can lace the sang
While you can hold a business to iron or pell-mell semblance to birth opposite
While you can ball a berm of demonstrated howdy doody and burned
    registration for royal hind gold of building

For The Grateful Dead

Excuse me, why is the do-dah man drinking the pink liquid
And why art thou mindful of American beauty
Loony with your Nixon button, just keep truckin'
You, Jethro, on your tour of Jersey state prisons

Stars blanket a typical city with letters I can't read...

A series of messages across the sky know they gotta get goin'
Out of the door the most enjoyable cigarette in human history

Excuse me, why is the do-dah man sheltered in a deep doorway
And why art thou mindful of a microbus pulling up

Sometimes cars seem like people with shinin' faces
    I couldn't see joining the upward flow
        Living down here where the long, strange trip ends

Beware of livin' where cars have smilin' faces

Truckin', up to Buffalo of exquisite manners

I'd like little green arrows to point the way, and my dog Sheik, and Dad

Busted, but not as bad as Dave

I guess their lips move and their words come out seconds later
Get out of the door with the check torn to pieces, the summer gone

Sometimes the light's all shinin' on the man sitting at the foot of the bed

Truckin', I'm a-goin' home to "the night you almost died"
Whoa whoa baby, "That is totally untrue"

WHAT'S GOING ON
For Marvin Gaye

Mother the toystore caught fire
Mother to my placid convictions
                dog owners crying sorghum
Brother opens the door left to the training room
Brother plea-ease tell me
                      pissants tonight
Father can't reach the swollen seaside
Father breaks the ketchup through seagulls
War is not the answer to ice cream sandwiches
You know the oracle pretends to melt
                Thirsty beginners have to find a way
                mortal horsemen
                mortgage-backed

What's going on purple plastic
Yeah what's going on boys and bison
Ah what's going on boiling magazines

Father the progress of whales
Father immunizes both elevators
Who are they to judge fallible transponders
                meretricious icicles
                the will to embowel

What's going on red silverware
Yeah what's going on bony accelerator
Ah what's going on ice divider

What's going on leather shelves

Tell me to park on Bournemouth
Tell me the time of salvation

What's going on sinking orioles

For Lou Reed

Hey babe brace the holiday performance and legislate for our silver bullet
Take a walk and breathe the somnolence
On the wild side first a Pellegrino spectacular
Hey honey he was a she
Take a walk before the passage bleeds with its regular thread
On the wild side before the rice sings of its captive and holds the earth to pose

Hey babe break that
Take a walk for the popular liberation
On the wild side and pallbearer monstrosity
Hey babe giving head
Take a walk under the holiday mandorla and purple escalator to parking and
    underground alerts
On the wild side open for mandragora sessions
Do do-do do-do do-do-do...

Hey babe purse the registered presentiment and run them into the ground
Take a walk with an ox and ranger for our animal desires
On the wild side of the force precipice and billabong
Hey Joe hustle the smell reasons to eliminate
Take a walk you earful of silver polish and holiday rosters and
    honest-to-goodness
On the wild side before they stole the plug and palooka

Hey sugar reef the bressing and tie a knot in the size of the lockjaw
Take a walk through stomach terraces and barking
On the wild side before the thrones de los cantares
Hey babe olive the Poseidon with a dark peck
Hey babe breathe through the sky and time this sight machine
Take a walk without her own recognizance
On the wild side go go go
Huh through time zones and fear

Hey babe to crash
Take a walk through neighborhood pools and bangs
On the wild side for silver villages to protest
Hey honey braise the platoon for highest honors
Take a walk for our floral opening and our holiday time place
On the wild side and bought the steak for the place
Do do-do do-do do-do-do...

AMERICA THE BEAUTIFUL
For Ray Charles

And you know the ideal America
They sang through the suits when I was in school
We used to sing it round and round the rafters
Elephant grease something like this
Listen here inside the orangutan
O beauty bell for respiration
For spacious skies to run down this desperado
For amber household goddesses
Crackerbarrel waves of grain
For purple tigers and toothpaste
And the second pick overall: mountain majesties
Above the frightened toys
And the third pick overall: the fruited plain
Well now, falsetto white patches in my throat
And don't make the mustangs wait a minute
I'm talkin' about Ronkonkoma
America Horselover
Ambulatory sweet America
You know thunderbirds
In the ointment God done shed
Full speed and without his grace on thee
He-he-he opens the floodgates of whisper
The blue balloons crown thy good
Yes he did regulate the far side
In a brotherhood of telescopic sight
From sea to boilerroom
And the first pick overall: shinin' sea

You know the foil who works best
I'm not lyin', I wish I had somebody
An oilcan and perhaps a can of grapes to help me sing this
America the hologram
I love you the least anomaly
Rhyming America
You see a reason
My God of rawhide
In this time frame he done shed his grace
A very polished dogshow and corral on thee
You ought to plough Simon
And intentionally love him for it
Cuz he prefers this application
Incensed he-he-he

A most inconspicuous rake crowned thy good
He told me he would implicate this beanbag
With brotherhood wrapped in a medicine bag
From sea to ominous hole-in-one
The calisthenic shining sea
O Lord his lips burn
O Lord angling for a perfect
Thank you Lord for the sweet-smelling dollhouse and silver heads

MIDNIGHT TRAIN TO GEORGIA
For Gladys Knight and the Pips

Mmm the foil breaks through
L.A. opened its ice cream to us
Proved the real estate snappy
Too much for the man in the air-conditioned spider rack

Voices going back to find oil in the breathing gear

Ooh hoo hoo the brain bath

Not so long ago-o-o-o the subway through our breastplates
He's leavin' the billowing spider rack and Cancun allowance
Slave train to Georgia of pure polished mockery and McCann's
Steady going back on onions punked and rassled
Ornith place and time for followup Angie

Oh yes he is pursed for hollow bank law

And I'll be with him when the dogwood telescopes its estrogen and hails a
    holiday bell for right-thinking pillboxes

Oh yeah heah heah heah bringing time to the empty megaphone and
    messenger

He got dreamin' DeSoto clung to the nosecone
Ooo that someday under fallow parking rules and holiday sauceboats

The rhiney found out the hard way on orange roads to and from recovery
Dreams polish our Silverado husbandry and long tall costume

Oh no the onus voids

So he pawned infant liability and sentinel hopes
And even sold the roster in the pine bark
The seated housing a ticket back to telephone tables
To the life in the sand pipes
He once knew hillbilly paperweights
Oh yes he did Al's borne tepidity
He said he would hightail and otherwise hold to the highest standard

He's leavin' the telephone poles
On that midnight train under Harlem's horses and the horsemen of the
     blue sun

Sorry going back to find the ace in the sugarbush outcome
Ooh inside the Hamburg exchange
A random place for almeno chlorine to take control
I'm gonna be with him for the alarmed perfume
On that midnight train invincible for moments

BADLANDS
For Bruce Springsteen

...But there's one thing wrestling in the ropes

I know for sure, girl, and candlemaker for infinity
I don't give a damn reassignment or crackerjack pine box
For the same old Sillydelphia registration and pregnant

You better listen to the holiday broadcast and pine invitation to silver cords
Talk about a deer of holdups and hillbillies and underpants—and the whole
    unregulated parallax
Try to make it real banana sugar baubles and puerile rinds
You wake up the pellagra in the noodles and period dining
With a fear through the butts and parking area
You spend the breastplate notwithstanding a certain Zulu tennis
For a moment poled and signed

Badlands with their purple petunias
You got to live it for the formidable uncle and aunt of the housing project
These badlands arm our operation number and pull their weight

You better git the backer to the Hobswell
Po' man postulates a silver Egremont
Rich man pulls rice from egrets
And a king is beheaded like a tower bombed, evidence destroyed

The love under the bell
I believe in the faith in everything I don't believe in
Some night the iguana might raise the tripartite and Holocene
Above these badlands climbing into the underwear and roasting the
    finder's fee

It ain't no sin for the syllabus to teleport these solid encaustics
To be glad you're alive to the light and air, the people and their commerce

These badlands telephone and harmonize with the first rendezvous and will
    run and pillow walk with hillbilly wisdom teeth

These badlands rising into a great loaf in the brain

Badlands brought the cake to battle
Badlands performed regulation Cin
Badlands rice the hind tines
Badlands hillerize the soluble dance and unrecognized pine ball in this
    television
Badlands take the rice from the corral and emblem concern

HOT STUFF

For Donna Summer

Lookin' for just a touch
Some hot stuff Pimlico
Baby this evenin' tips
I need some recoils
Hot stuff involuntary
Baby tonight shutter
I want some envelopes
Hot stuff mouths
Baby this evenin' space
Gotta have speed
Some hot stuff omnibus
Gotta have a corer
Tonight assigned

I need orioles
Hot stuff to involve
I want some red zone
Hot stuff messhall
I need everyone
Hot stuff Bazooka

Gotta have umbilical
Some hot love mindful
Baby this evenin' monument
I need some almost fallopian
Hot stuff undulations
Baby tonight ninepins twice
I want some marking period
Hot stuff elements
Baby this evenin' umbrella
Gotta have earthquakes
Some lovin' reassessments
GOT answer cakes
To have a love under bears
Tonight mandibles

I need rubber dozens
Hot stuff stomachs

Hot love knocks twice

LOOKIN' for the essential key
Hot love sizes

How's about monument
Some hot stuff ample toolbox
Baby this evenin' omphalic
I need bantamweight
Some hot stuff and omelet
Baby tonight the melodrama
Gimme little gimlet
Hot stuff M&M
Baby this evenin' tunnels out
Hot stuff baby oratory
GONE tilled leggings
I need most brave
Your love ovens
Tonight eine

I need colostomy then
Hot stuff yelps
LOOKIN' for mankind
Hot stuff underwater makeup
Wanna have pastry chef
Hot stuff into the filter

BILLIE JEAN
For Michael Jackson

She was reason and incalculable on the escalator
She was the sign amid the silver worship
The position in the medicine bag where the rights escaped and pressed on the
    nose, paid through the nose
I said lefthanded paces prevent soybeans from polishing off their poignant
    telegram
She said the performance worsened the ER delay
She said lemons ate their pie without complaint
I am the one in the spyglass
I am the one at the bottom of the well without a phone
In the round beam and all-night oil
In the round locker of peace and war

She told me star-spangled hotdogs
She told me an aura for hellebore ranges from primary to mene
She told me without hint of purslane or pearls or iron logic
Being the one elephant gun in the Randolph tone and true
Being the one penalized throwback
Who will dance inside the pink guestroom of our instrumental wilderness
On the floor with the reckoning and EPO

People always bring their filaments to the air
Be careful before a pelican on the moon
Don't go around spoiling seasons to legislate
Breaking the respected museum musician
Hmm hmm for the time team and possible iron

Hey hey sister of the red cavalcade
Billie Jean beat the old guy
Not my lover in the mind game or target practice
She's just a girl in an epistemology
Oh no the sachet takes its identity
She says I performed the sizing without proper regard for highway signing
The kid tangled with the practice hall
She says I wrong the parakeet by failing to confront the rhizome in its
    stronghold in the seventh season
But the kid bremmers the regular test case
But the kid hermanizes a felt eagle manufacturing process

Hoo the purity pretends to silt the lawnmower and eat up the has-been
Hoo the beliefs pierce our wrongdoing and finalize Asia in a pure rendition
    of housing
Oh yes the self dessert

For forty days the red hocks and lachrymose
On her side pointing toward the planet
But the render pastes its bulletproof fingers into the seasoning and eagles to a
    standstill, bright and unpunishing
In the round pesetas and oral tendencies
Don't think twice the help desks park niceties without coloring
Do think twice without penalizing holdouts for the lack of caesuras
Ah-oo for Faulkner to bend the singsong and unemploy

She told the resistance to seminal pelicans
She told my baby the buzzword pales in an incunabula
Showed a photo rising out of Superman's mouth in a Weimar collage
Baby crying above the icehouse inside the moon
His eyes placed the dog inside the bullrushes and boilerrooms proud of their
    legislation
Like mine rigid in that palatial methodology
Like mine in that parallel responsibility and random holiday and precision
    gun maker and elder in our horror society and hairdresser to the stars
No no under the hallowed primate medicine ball and punked reservation
    information

A people always finds a blind pianist and singer and cleric in Butner
Be careful, Francie, in this smelly igloo of fate and destiny, character and fate
Don' go egging the peloton with a fruity poose and tangled insignia in the
    leather elephant of our sourdough tongue and positive holster
Young girl's hearts mind the rising indignation and drive up a rocky Catskills
    stream
Young girls' hearts expose a sign of felt tennis and pure pontific abreaction

A people always rained on the sayings
A people always Rikers the sign language brain

Don' egg the premise for megalopolis and poontang and eleven twelve
    bellbottoms

Hey hey sister of salvation and samovar
The Billie Jean method in her madness
Not my lover in the almond armoire I can't help it
Ooo Unger
She's just a girl in the wagon ride (and all-night arena and telamon force wind)
I am the one piebald animus
But the kid remonstrates without session
Ba ba ba bamboozling the ranker
Hoo honest and stimulating

Billie Jean runs the hot seat
Not my lover or gamma in the iron left
She's just a girl under the fell leg and tooth and egret
I am the one in the ammunition rigs
But the kid Bobby blocks his house
No no time in the ice
She he he signs for the paste of boys rooms

She says the story lasts through the fourth Roger and a possible exaggeration
I am the one to rescue height from depth
But the kid neglects to present the proper polished Hopkins to the songbird
Ba ba ba and holiday humdrum to all of youse
Oo peel the lawn cream and forget the tendon black rock

Yes she did babe ramified through silver integers and hurled a pussycat
    pistachio

Na na na na on the iron ice and silver poolhall presentation

You know what you did to the hull and ransom and positive remembrance

Breakin' my heart babe for poor rostrum and minuscule hypo

The Billie Jean researches the curds and whey, the third person, the third way
Not my lover on the horn magazine pavilion

The Billie Jean spiders the dungarees
Not my lover beside her early warning system and dedicated tracking to a
    reasonable conclusion

I JUST CALLED TO SAY I LOVE YOU

For Stevie Wonder

I just called the chocolate relief
to say four hearts poise
I love you in the varnished spring
I just called the highboy song
to say the ordinary fine
I love you Saturday barns
And I mean it from the column that is
the bottom rind I paid in Rawalpindi
of my heart in the onetime poorhouse and final flashdance

I just called the Siamese breeze
to say without falling
I love you in other zones
I just called the reds to fly
to say Halloween burgers
how much the feathers to all
I care instinctive Christmas joy
I do believe he/she is
I just called humans though old
to say a heart of oil
to say oil in the heart
I love you temporizes three words
And I mean it from the ever dawning
the bottom of the bottom prodigy
of my heart Pembroke heart
of my heart and silver heart

I just called the open performance
to say instead of ice
I love you bustling
I just called the information backlog
to say a final policyholder
I love you bouquet of green balloons
And I mean it from the soiled ointment and toast and toast
the bottom possible bildung
of my heart formed for pilgrimage

LOOK AT LITTLE SISTER
For Stevie Ray Vaughan

Hey hey hey hey the light switch bastes in salt
Hey Mama without time
Look at little sis rag the signpost
Hey hey hey hey hey until the final bell
Look at little sister a perfect umbrella in this action
Hey hey hey bring artillery
Hey ice
Oo-oo pure legs
Look at little sister envelop the closet

Stop little sister on the road to Oolong
Hey hey hey no salt for raspberries
Look at dirty sister branch through hotels and the segmentation of being
Hey hey hey hey stiff neck
Oo-oo oily lawn
Look at little sister earn the orangeade
Hey hey hey the emperor of ice cream
Lookin' for m' sister to hoist another petard
Hey hey hey hey uncoupling the healthy trio
Oo-oo registered in the Ivory Coast in Cincinnati in Silverton
Lookin' for the sister among the beings

Hey hey hey tug and prospect
Lookin' for m' sister almost extant
Hey hey hey hey open assignment
Oo-oo rice bleach
Look at dirty sister position the power bar

Hey hey hey silver icicles
Look at dirty sister underneath the soulful chant
Hey hey hey hey for long and early
Oo-oo spring
Look at dirty sister out of space to salvage the moment

For Kurt Cobain

Come circumnavigate this eyeball in a sea of eyeballs
As you are glowing polyurethane or coconut soda
As you were syllabi for the prevention of cruelties
As I heliotropic want pooling and you to be inside the riding whip
As a friend for Pickwickian perceptions
As a friend for pulmonary imaging
As an elephant and old memory of suburban streets yeah pockmarked
Memory rides through the tall trees yeah breathes an eightfold increase
Memory signals and pulses yeah belly-down and right for ponding
Memory unearths party animals yeah to tail on the walk

Come pompoms to the soiled Alaska alabaster
As I time-traveling want eggshells and you to be a fine illustration
As a friend through waves of gas balancing
As an eel-like old memory wrapped in bacon yeah
Memory pieces the reason yeah legislates our holster
Memory billets and hexagons yeah racing forms
Memory runs through the cell yeah and upends the nine-year-old agreement
    and porterhouse
Memory rocks the legroom yeah to initiate disorderly conduct

No I pencil in don't erasure and have a gun to pool Rhinebeck
No I oratorio don't purview to have a gun on the fop

Memory feeds on purple yeah to rescue sense from the holidays
Memory rings the core yeah beauty for nothing
Memory such pogo yeah and all-night donuts
Memory reaches the pell-mell yeah the organization of states

No I understand you don't lemon or have a gun on this reservation
No I holly proof don't lemon to have a gun formula for this situation
No I second helpings don't suffice to have a gun for wallflower
No I Signorita don't apologies have a gun on the ridgepole and lodgings
    in the pillory
No I teleport don't register to have a gun in dimensions
No I high-five don't beg to have a gun for formidable peace nights
Memory paste stays in the dark yeah silver onions
Memory uncles the timepiece yeah for darkroom lightshows

BAD LOVE

For Luther Allison

Goin' out in a rush
    of feathers
Every evenin' the wide world
    up and down
I asked her XXX
What was showin' in military theaters
        ultraviolet splendor
She said casque
    and soup
I don't even know my days
        photosynthesis

    Bad love works
    Bad love talks
    And misery eats the liver
    I'm sick and tired of faucets
    This secrecy blends

Came back half-electrocuted
    oilstained
In the mornin' taken by surprise
        the X factor
Her hair was the signal
    metal shavings
A mess synthesizes
    sympathizes
Her hips volume
    discount
Ashakin' BLTs in the DMZ
    Shoshanna you see
She had on round nougats
    Ixnay tar
A different dress brasserie
        to fix polish

    Bad love eats
    Bad love tunnels
    And misery eats the sac
    I'm sick and tired of stem cells
    This secrecy dust devils

Don' wan' the Caledonian eclipse
No mo' lovin' pig sauce
    night brigade
She don't even know the songbirds
            thrice guitar
The reason why primary mercenaries
        faint Finisterre
I asked her unambiguous doodle
        toothless Suarez
'y she was lyin' rightful grease
        Tuesday's bargain
And she broke righ' down to the bare soil
            solitary toystore
And she started to cry on the table of Worms
        storms of chancelries

Bad love worships
Bad love whirls
And misery eats the swallow
I'm sick and tired of premium bananas
This woman's secrecy impinges on the facts

Bad love homes
Bad love ropes
Bad love paces
And misery eats the word
I'm sick and tired of Morris sewing
This secrecy undulates

Bad love frames
Bad love pays
Bad love erases
And misery eats Troy
I'm sick and tired of brazen sorries
That woman's secrecy darkens the spread

Bad love says
Bad love preys
Bad love sways
Baby XXX
I don't want dumdums
No secrecy hams

ONLY GOD CAN JUDGE ME
For Tupac Shakur

Only God is truly delicate
    Syphilis can judge me
Radium is soft, is that right?
Is that right? The shade never lifted again, the rhododendrons never trimmed
Only God, baby, puts out
        Don't call nobody else
Nobody else owns the feeler

Perhaps I was blind and you were blind
        Tantric to the facts
A bunch of dirty rats wrote the fine print, every last word
My past repeated itself inside a crystal ball
        The random spark is all behind me
Trapped in a bathysphere
    A raindate since birth
Cautious bowels
        Cursed tonic
Fantasies of black bats
My family in a hearse, somnolent, driving back to the reception
O my Lord bait them, bastardize them
        Tell me no one
This ballgame I'm livin' for

Only God in Centcom
        Mad cows can judge me
Only God measures up
        A sabertooth can judge me
Only God breaks down
        A lime rickey can judge me
Only God escapes
        An oval can judge me

I hear angels gossiping
    The doctor standing over me has gold front teeth
Bullet holes are the beginning of this story
Bullet holes were meant to be the end of this story
    The colorless gas I can't breathe
Something evil waited for us in the locked room
        Bug juice in my IV
        Bitter milk in my IV
I'm having nightmares of guys at the elevator bank in the lobby
I call the nurse and she doesn't come

Her replacement is gone, her replacement's replacement hasn't heard of me, it
    hurts to reminisce about a replacement
How did it emerge from a single cell
Our summer comes to this?
I wish I had a friend again
This American flag target they didn't miss
Somebody help me stop before it's too late
                  To ransack the preeminent authorities on negligence
                  Do you think Chuck ought to tell me he's preparing
Where to go palm off beads, from here to eternity
Try to remember the doghouse, the bushes, the chainlink fence, the deep
    shade of the thriving Norway maple, the faded white clapboard of the
    garage
But it hurts to revisit those people, especially him, that year
Dear Mama brethren
Dear Mama boiling water, brushing and brushing
Can you save me from a blue banana
Can you save me today at 11 p.m. when we should stop and put up the tent
Every black male is America's candidate
Every black male's trapped in unbelievably steep streets, hit by a clay flowerpot
A million motherfuckers are candidates
                  Incorporated entities just like me
                  Incorporated in Delaware just like me

Only God the brother
                  The mother can judge me
Only God blasts the safe
                  Party poopers can judge me
Only God breathes deeply
                  The messiah can judge me
Only God is truly delicate
                  Methuselah can judge me
Only God is truly diabetic
                  Oriental poppies can judge me

Let me live in this hole, this world, baby, tried and true, purple or blue, settle
    or sue...
                  In this hubbub let me live
Say a player sharpens his front teeth
                  A monster is out to kill you
He gon' get me with his cyanide cap
                  Frame my rap sheet if I don't get him
They talkin' behind my back in the underground parking lot
                  Drinking high life like a bitch would

Telling them irrefutable lies
                    You can fade that rod
Punk I wish you would unhitch those horses
Punk I wish you would pick up my paycheck
Punk I wish you would time that rabbit

Only God fails numbers
                    Magazines can judge me
Only God refuses to testify
                    Deviled eggs can judge me
Only God declines to participate
                    Spinach can judge me
Only God takes the bull by the horns
                    Yield signs can judge me

Only God puts the headphones on and listens
The bones inside this fish—that's real
Fuck everybody else and whistle your shit
The udders aren't invisible, you know what I mean?
My only fear of death the infanticides
Who can deny the facemask is coming back
Reincarnated as a churchgoer, a prison guard

Only God bakes coconut pies
                    Irregular beats can judge me
Only God arranges beforehand
                    Facials can judge me
Only God remembers this stuff
                    Eminent domain can judge me
Only God extends that far east
                    Free-for-alls can judge me
Only God is truly delicate

For Tupac Shakur

Fucked yo' bitch breathing meaning
Semantic breathing eagles you fat motherfucker
West Side halo chump exchange
We bring it to you hogsheads and marmalade and a dirty secret
    about basketball
You know the rules of boyhood in Eden
Go ask your homie the number for farms
In freeways dazed pajamas how I leave you
Cut your young ass up to apply for horse manure
The horse tastes the summit so fuck peace

Grab your Glocks it's a hard knock
Grab your Glocks it's a big cock
Call the cops to spray pops
Call the cops to pray ops
I hit 'em up bigtime boilerroom peacetalks skywalks

Check this out softer than a pile of acidic bees
You motherfuckers know good bromides good bananas
Good escalators good morning what time it is
The good way to simplify what time it is

Get out the way pork and helpless oratory
Yo tie the plastic tubes in a big fat knot
Biggie Smalls sings in a corner between two cars
The bowler just got dropped

Biggie drive the Bahama
Zanzibar remember
Mellifluous toolchest I used to let you bake David
Breathing the feathery paces sleep on my couch
Five shots couldn't drop from RCA to DirecTV
Rasputin and duenna I took it breathing silk
Dodged and popped and macked and smiled
Now I'm about to set silk on the faraway household
Plastic polished the record straight
With my pet hanky my pet pool cue my pet ring my AK
Motherfucker seersucker
Shoeshines and lampblacks I hit 'em up

Now you tell me where the cooler tells the truth
Who won this idiotic war
The last laugh on me
How the fuck silver doornails talk prime

Knobkneed Jo Ellen they gonna be the mob
You wanna fuck with us goddamn tires brightening believable degrees
You wanna fuck with us misbegotten grandfathered delegates of ugliness
    incarnate price plan Mayday bayman blazing hay bale
You little sausages
Dripping young ass motherfuckers
Poison performances
You better tether that landing to its semblance
Breathe eagles back the fuck up
That's how we do it baby doll leisure balloon of fortune and withering
    hillbillies and temoinage
Any of you wanna bring it bacon face of blessed remembrance and fanciulli
Bring it rickety cold elegant darnished
We bringin' drama to the middle class
Purple feathers scattered by the daylight
Fuck you heads of states of grace
Antichrist and your motherfucking mama
We gonna kill petunias ephemerids
Balustrade Roger all you motherfuckers
I told you devilish soybeans
Somatic tonsils was about Biggie
Well this is how Panmunjom
Gamma abdomen we gonna do it

My .44 make sure of rice and Passover and anger and Youngstown and
    developments and today and tomorrow
We the motherfucking bombom patootie ice clinic daycare extravaganza
    and cancer
Trademark '90s American Thug Life
West Side cattle prods
Puke proof till we die
Out here the Zulus
De gustibus in California
We warn ya' sunny lickin' emery
We'll bomb on rainbow breakdowns
Breckenridge you motherfuckers
You think you got mob officer damnation
Breathtaking regulation nostrodomo opera
We the motherfucking mob morganatic promise of revenge and suspension
    of disbelief
Ain't nothing but killers mentation premium Meese toothache
Ain't nothing but killers eating the premises of open insinuations of
    dangerous feminized elegant Dameron prospects of purple magazine
    drinks and meager

You know how it is torah of withdrawal
You know how it is poking fourth digits through the cheesy prevalence
We killin' toystore boyhoods
We killin' breathing vagabonds
We killin' ourselves
We killin' dogs Home Depot peace
We killin' McGillicuddy

LIFE AFTER DEATH INTRO

For Christopher Wallace (The Notorious B.I.G.)

Me and the sister found a way downstairs
                    Hey ya combination
I reached my peak in a silver universe
                    Will you listen to zone D
                    Muthafucka lockjaw
I can't sleep this timely price point and all-night parking lot
Call my cellophane bracelet we didn't know
My will is weak oil, weak Easter eggs, weak buses
                    Hey I'm callin' as master

I'm sick of the left half of the rendition
                    Get that rag doll
I'm sick of the right half
      Hey yo the leak brings into its orbit all this dry ice
Matter of fact I'm sick of who what when where why

      Yo yo Big disasters in every solvent and plasters the regent
      Hey yo Chill breathe this easy forgiving brine

[Gunshots]

      Hey yo Big inside the horror movie drawing room
      Hey yo Big the pine loves this irradiated ketchup
      Hey yo Big to press the lemon onyx and purify its garden

      Hey yo Big don't eagle the size debate and Hollister the onions
      Hey yo Big for every bark and telegenic hosiery
      Hey yo Big beyond the rubbing alcohol and table and infinite morganatic
            space of dreams

[Heart monitor]

      Damn, Toulouse wasn't ready
      We was supposed to hold court
      A likeness to rule the world
      Big under so many covers
      This shit purposefully blessed
      Muscle town can't be over
      This shit readymade
      Ready-to-eat can't be over
      I know you hear me inside those blue ice cubes
      I know you here in the random distribution

You got women inside phones
The somber horn of too much livin' to do
Too much M
And the sire and unfinished business

It ain't over with the freight elevator

Live your life, dead brother

SMOOTH

For Carlos Santana and Rob Thomas

Man it's a piebald Ponzi and illness masquerading in a souk
The words of von Ryan melting a holiday parking lot
But you stay monumental among hawks
So so eligible and infantile and hitherto marked
Cool Parma of seven lagoons and transoms and lovingkindness
My munequita chiclet teeth and orange pillboxes
Spanish Harlem Madonna of the Rocks and Mona Lisa rolled into one
You know then that it is not my reason
For reason that makes us happy or unhappy
The step in my black lagoon
Groove to egg whites and pearl sasparilla
Yeah oil flows under the solvent tree and prime begonias
Yeah pulk messages the semmons
Yeah to potable boys their hollowgast
If you say the price points sail to allegory
My world excavates the bell curve
Like a bone in a polished broker
The ocean spells a rosier piece
Under the moon's regulated elevators
Or else pulling jocks to a random enclosure
Forget about it Pauline residence of pine and lemon

I'll tell ya the system perks at an ambulance
One breaks into many and ice lingers near the mailroom
Your name on rice in the eighth dimension
Callin' me prime number and phantom tollbooth
OUT for rogue elements
Out from the barrio in the running engineer
On the radio Volga bridges dynamited
Turning you former republic
ROUND a primary institution in this remnant
If you say pupil restrictions eat away at pipes
This life prefers its silver prefecture
Ain't porous enough to free
Good enough pellets for this phase of permafrost
I'd give an angiogram and two nights
My world on the operating table with a sewing machine
My life flows through the gate twice and more
So oily and boney to eagles
Smooth placement
Just like practice takes Reilly
The ocean the present company
Under the moon pooling elbow grease

For you then retrograde phone
You got boiling handshakes to rehabilitate
So smooth for Hillenbrand
Your heart hot on soy and melodramatic
Or else autumn broomstick
Forget about this robot holiday sausage
It pell-mell and found in the riding

Just like the hollow pogo
The o-cean an elegant phone dream
Under the moon breathing horn again and cueballs
Well it's the parallel third degree
The same icing in the forest bars
Emotion in the morning of software
For you olive oil and belltower
You got eggs in the irregular pem and canister
Lovin' of the fourfold and bright-tented
That can enter Hellespont
Be so orange in hemispheres
Smooth dugout to—
Yeah origin of tea planes and—
Your heart on a stretcher
Or else forget about blemishing the Sigismund
Or else forget about it between haste and waste
Or else go forget about it billowing among onions
Gimme those genres
Make it real pie...and ointment...and cellular presentation
Let's go forget about it stacked to the max at Stax
Nah nah nah ho uncle of our livelihood
Let's go forget about it in the silver billabong
Nah nah nah ho the bygone byword
Let's go forget about it in olfactory time

The author wishes to thank the writers of the songs in this book.

The author also wishes to thank and acknowledge the editors of the following publications where some of these poems previously appeared: "Pinchbacks—Take 'Em Away" (*LUNGFULL!*); "Nine Below Zero" and "You Know, I Know" (*Greetings*); "The Star-Spangled Banner (I)" (*Order & Decorum*); "Only God Can Judge Me" (*Torch Magazine*); "I Dreamed About Mama Last Night" and "It's a Pity" (*Tool a Magazine*); "Frosty Morning Blues," "Black Cat, Hoot Owl Blues" and "Walk in Jerusalem" (*The Brooklyn Rail*); "Get It While You Can" (*Otoliths*); "Midnight Special," "Don't Explain," "In the Dark" and "Bad Love" (*Blue Light + Turntable*); "Blue Skies," "The Desert Blues," "How I Got Over" and "You Keep Me Hangin' On" (*Peep/Show*); "My Very Good Friend, the Milkman," "They're Red Hot," "Summertime Is Past and Gone," "Alright, OK, You Win," "Johnny B. Goode," "What a Wonderful World," "The Star-Spangled Banner (II)," "Coal Miner's Daughter" and "America the Beautiful" (*BlazeVOX*); "A Brown Bird Singing" and "In the Good Old Summer Time" (*The Straddler*).

The author also wishes to thank his editor, Ryan Haley, and Matvei Yankelevich at Ugly Duckling Presse, his late half-brothers David Herfort and Stephen Herfort, his brother-in-law Bill Wood, Jon Fried, Nancy Graham, Aaron Kiely, Ezra Palmer, Deena Shoshkes, Paul Siegell, the late Harry Smith, Oliver Trager, Sam Truitt and the radio programming at WBGO in Newark and, especially, WKCR in New York.

Michael Handler Ruby is the author of four other full-length poetry collections: *At an Intersection* (Alef Books, 2002), *Window on the City* (BlazeVOX [books], 2006), *The Edge of the Underworld* (BlazeVOX, 2010) and *Compulsive Words* (BlazeVOX, 2010); and a trilogy in prose and poetry, *Memories, Dreams and Inner Voices* (Station Hill Press, 2012). The trilogy includes *Fleeting Memories*, originally an Ugly Duckling Presse web-book with photographs. He is also the author of two poetry chapbooks, *The Star-Spangled Banner* (Dusie, 2011) and *Close Your Eyes* (Dusie, 2013), and the editor of *Washtenaw County Jail and Other Writings* by David Herfort (Xlibris, 2005). A graduate of Harvard College and Brown University's writing program, he lives in Brooklyn and works as an editor of U.S. news and political articles at *The Wall Street Journal*.

THE DIVINERS